ROADMAP
TO
ENLIGHTENMENT

A GUIDEBOOK TO FINDING
YOUR TRUE SELF

DR. MINH VO

ISBN: 978-0-9815258-0-8 (trade cloth)
First Edition, May 2008
Lisa Tran – Editor, Art Director
Nancy Lee – Cover Design
Brandon Gillam – Illustrations

CONTENTS

CHAPTER I

CREATION

It was getting very late and dark outside, but she could still hear the sound of her neighbors moving around through the thin walls that separated their small one bedroom apartment. She didn't know what sounded louder, the neighbors' rustling or her husband who lay there sound asleep, exhausted and snoring. As annoying as it all sounded, it really didn't matter. All she could think about was *eight more days*, just a little over a week, and counting until the day her life would completely be changed forever. She thought back to the time her doctor first gave her the test results and sharing the news with her husband. Initial responses of shock, fear, and denial raced through both their minds. But now the pain in her lower back, which had steadily increased over the last four or five months, caused her to toss and turn a little extra tonight. Feeling hot, uncomfortable and restless, she finally found the magical position that allowed her enough relief to give her mind a rest from the pain. She slowly drifted off to sleep.

Around seven the next morning, damp sheets and wetness in her pajama bottoms woke her up. Initially, she wondered whether she wet the bed. Was there something seriously wrong? Was it water? Was it blood? She quickly got up and saw that her pad was drenched with tinges of blood, but that was perhaps normal for her current state. So, she simply cleaned up and began her morning ritual. After starting the coffee maker, she began preparing a little toast to help combat the habitual nausea she'd experienced since this all began. The difference with this day in particular was that within minutes, her pad was soaked once again. She became increasingly worried that there was something seriously wrong and immediately called her doctor's emergency line. Her doctor simply replied, "It sounds like your water broke. Wake your husband up right away and come to the hospital. You're about to have your first baby."

Birth, the creation of a human being, is a wondrous and mysterious occurrence that can be joyful yet terrifying when experienced for the very first time. It is as much of a rite of passage for the child being born into this world as it is for the parents that created the child. This expression of a union between a male and a female, as well as a union of the spirit and the human body, brings about the reason why we are here in the first place: *life*. And yet, most of us born into this world really have no idea how we got here, and what it is we are supposed to do once we arrive. Have you ever wondered how or why life began? Where did we come from? Why are we here? And where do we go when we pass away? With everything in life, we know there exists a beginning and an end. What once had existed or still exists on this Earth was created from something, changes over time, and eventually lives out its physical existence, only to fade away into memories or possibly back to which it came: the source of creation.

Not only is there great variety in life on Earth, there are also many responses to the life that we experience. For some people, the emotions leading up to parenthood can be joy, happiness, excitement, exhilaration, amazement, and anticipation; others feel fear, anger, apprehension, denial, worry, and anxiety. We all make choices and react differently to similar events and experiences. What creates our unique emotions, responses, perceptions, and attachments to experiencing the same event that billions of people for generations have already experienced, and why? What drives each individual to move through life's experiences so differently from one another? If we understood these questions, do we have a chance to consciously point ourselves in a different direction? Have you ever woken up and wondered how you got to where you are in life? How much of your life is lived consciously or unconsciously? How much of it is driven by your automatic actions, emotions, habits, or your unconscious beliefs—the things that cause you to go into auto-pilot?

Within every person's life there exists a mother, father, race, culture, heritage, and a lineage that is perceived as the uniqueness and identity of the individual. But if we turn back the clock of time, erasing one's life, one's family, one's country, one's civilization, one's planet, one's universe, back to the point of what many of us call "creation," all we would have left is *nothing*. What was once considered as *something* in existence began as *nothing*. How can something come from nothing? What came first, the chicken or the egg? This then poses the question of evolution versus creation. Was it a big bang or was it God? Or could it have been both? And if God exists, then who is he or she, and what was before God? What existed in the very beginning and how do we fit in the grand scale of things? These questions have plagued many of us in our lives at one time or another. Some of us turn to science for explanations, while others turn to religion and philosophy for something to believe in.

The Christian bible states that God created the existence of life, the planets, moons and the stars that make up our universe. He created man, who created the suffering of sin. The bible teaches that through the life of Jesus Christ (God incarnate), God as human overcame the pains and temptations, the suffering of mortal man's sins. Jesus' death and resurrection was God showing his grace and sacrifice for the atonement of man's sins that grants us the ability to receive salvation and heaven. Buddhist philosophy teaches us that our physical life is not real, that life is the transient intolerance of physical and mental suffering—dukkha. Suffering is created through our attachments to ego's emotional desires of life and the world around us. By rejecting the ego of our humanly desires, we free ourselves from mental illusion. We are to reject the illusion that we mentally create from our life experiences in order to get to a place of silence, a place of "nothing," a place from which life originated—thus we awaken to enlightenment. Both of these teachings are older paradigms of consciousness evolvement that rely on the path of rejection. They ask you to reject your emotions, desires, temptations, sins, the mind, the ego, in essence rejecting your entire physical experience and its existence. Why?

Christianity, Buddhism, Islam, Hinduism, Taoism, and Judaism each have their own version of how life began and our role within it. This leads us to the question, "Which one is right?" Have you tried to seek the truth for yourself? Have you explored religion after religion only to wind up feeling even more lost and confused? Have you chosen one religion as your foundation, but mix and match others to make the answers to God or life itself more meaningful? Or have you given up on religion, perhaps chosen the path of science? Do you choose to believe in nothing, or call it spirituality, simply because religion, philosophy, or whatever, is simply frustrating and unexplainable? Are you ready to explore a new paradigm of consciousness evolvement, one of unconditional acceptance?

Let's probe and examine the mysteries and secrets of creation and the human spirit by tracing back the footprints of many masters of the past, to unlock the teachings that have been misinterpreted or misunderstood over time. By demystifying and connecting separated teachings from the past, filling in gaps of understanding and explaining these spiritual teachings in current language and understanding, my hope is to help you come to know who you really are and guide you to understanding your own full potential within yourself. As Master

Jesus stated in John 14:12, "I tell you the truth, anyone who has faith in me will do what I have been doing. He will do even greater things than these." Similarly, Master Buddha stated, "All living beings have the Buddha nature and can become Buddha." Master Lao Tzu stated, "The great Way is easy, yet people prefer the side paths. Be aware when things are out of balance. Stay centered within the Tao." Although these masters originated in different countries, different eras of time, different cultures and each had a different language and approach to ways of life, yet they all reminded us of our human potential. Your potential is found within the mastery of who you are. It is not a dangling carrot beyond your reach, nor is it beyond your ability to conceive. Although each of these masters' statements are worded differently, they all tell us that the ability to reach enlightenment, salvation, or simply a state of higher consciousness is within all of us. You have the ability to experience your own potential and to know who you are and why you are here, regardless of your chosen religion, doctrine, or belief.

Are you ready to find out?

The science of evolution tells us that life on Earth began with water. Can life form from a single drop of water? Does water one day magically become a single living cell like that of an amoeba? Do a bunch of single cells decide to join together to create a fish, a bird, or a human being? When we look at life all around us, we see variation in everything. There is a seemingly infinite visual diversity, a plethora of colors, shapes, and sizes in incredible magnitudes. It is the evolution of creation that has provided these varieties of distinction and separation within existence, but these lines of separation and variations in creation become erased as we travel back in time to the point of no existence. All living species that exist today can be traced back to this origin, a single cell at its moment of conception. As we travel backwards in time, lines of separation and identity become lines of unity, the same unity of an egg and sperm that creates a child within the womb. These lines of separation unite to give birth to existence, starting with the creation of one cell. The union of lines that create existence itself is the same union that creates the human child, the spirit, the planets, and the stars. Today, these lines are being shown to us in the advanced sciences of quantum mechanics and quantum physics, as well as what theoretical physics call superstring theory. Science is beginning to unfold the genetic explanation and expression of God and who we are, as well as how it relates to the human spirit. Science is discovering that these lines of separation are created by magnetic vibrations or frequencies. When we compare two different religions and how they explain creation and our physical reality, we begin to see their relationship to science and vibrations today.

In examining Christian and Buddhist teachings, we find a link between creation and ourselves, and see how this knowledge can be applied to our everyday lives. When you come to understand the origins of creation, you understand where you came from, how you are connected to everything, and what your true spiritual potential is. When you understand the make up of the spirit and how it correlates to your physical life, you can align yourself with the potential of the magnetic vibrational field around you.

The Christian bible states in John 1:1-5, "In the beginning was the Word, and the Word was with God, and the Word was God. He was with God in the beginning. Through him all things were made; without him nothing was made that has been made. In him was life, and that life was the light of men. The light shines in the darkness, but the darkness has not understood it." When we first look at this scripture, it appears to be very simple and self explanatory, that "God" created everything. Let me propose that when we examine these words closely, they reveal something extremely different. It states that in the beginning was the "Word," that the "Word" came first and not "God." And *then* the "Word" was *with* "God," and then it *was* "God." Words are merely sound and sounds are various forms of vibrations that are created by combining different frequencies. Consider that "God" doesn't necessarily mean an all-powerful, mighty creator of all things, but possibly a meta-physical God that is made up of a conglomeration of vibrations or frequencies that created all things from the original vibration. Consider how these same frequencies are understood in quantum mechanics. The vibration of atoms creates matter through the acceleration of force, the same force that creates matter creates life itself, creates everything. "God" is the conglomeration of frequencies, the conglomeration of "all things that have ever been made."

Looking at Buddhism, it teaches us the path of detachment from the illusionary world of our thoughts and desires to awaken the state of enlightenment. This path uses conventional meditation to achieve silence within the mental mind in order to achieve a state of "no mind" and "no self," a state of nothingness from which existence began. Used in conjunction, the two Chinese characters that represent the word "enlightenment" translate as "beginning opened." Together, the foundation of Buddhist principles and this translation of the word show us a path that points us back to our true origin—nothingness, silence, no sound. In the beginning was silence and through sound or frequency, creation, and existence was then opened from the silence. This is on par with Christianity's explanation of how existence began.

Combining these two spiritual teachings we ask the question, what was before "God" or creation? The answer is vibrational frequency. This can be a very perplexing concept to grasp, but consider that when we experience nothing, we are still experiencing something. Ask yourself the question, "How do I know that I hear, see, feel, taste, or smell nothing?" The only way to know that nothing exists is to know that something exists—the contrast of *something* helps us know there is *nothing*. To hear nothing, see nothing, feel nothing, taste nothing, and smell nothing is simply determined by comparing it to something that does exist. This is the same something, or frequency, for which our five senses of the body are the receptors of the world around us. Within the gaps of silence or nothingness, we find the existence or expression of frequency, "God," and the origin of all existence and creation. When we combine these two very different religious teachings, they tell us a similar story of how life and existence began—the story of God, frequency, and creation.

Before there was life, there existed the great infinite eternal space that held a vibration. Consciousness existed within this vibration. Consciousness is the expression of infinite intelligence that offers the ability for creation and existence to form into infinite possibilities. When consciousness expanded, it brought forth new life in order to experience all the parts of itself and all there was to offer in this existence. As this vibration continued to expand, it moved and collided within itself and created matter out of different levels of vibrational frequency. This vibrational matter then took shape in the form of particles that created the planets, stars, and galaxies that make up the continually expanding vibration known as the universe. Within this universe, consciousness held and maintained the vibration of its own intelligence and wisdom, a "universal consciousness," in order to continue to grow and govern its own creation. It is this vibration, this universal consciousness that we want to return to and tap into, such that we can consciously experience the awareness of not only ourselves, but the divine vibration of creation within all of us.

Creation birthed variation for comparison and balance. It birthed the balance of dark versus light, positive versus negative, masculine versus feminine, yin versus yang, and the inception of creation, evolution, and reincarnation. As this vibration continued to expand, so did creation's need to experience itself within this vibration, bringing about the birth of separate vibrations in the form of spirit—a pure expression of the self, of who we really are. Variations provide measurement and comparison, in order to allow wisdom and discernment within the experience. To know the differences between variations is to understand intelligence.

This is similar to how we know the difference between morning and night. As the sky shifts from light to dark, we see and experience the many degrees of changes within the essence of its source—light.

The creation of the spirit from its vibration was our own variation from the Original Vibration. Just as a child is born into its human experience, we separated from the union of creation and the multitude of vibrational frequencies that makes up the totality which is God. This is the way we experience our own creation. As the Christian Bible states Genesis 1:26, "And God said, 'Let us make man in *our* image, after *our* likeness.'" God is not an individual, almighty powerful being, but is a conglomeration of who we were before we came into our physical life. We created the spirit in order to experience our whole creation, beginning with the inception of the self, and will always remain connected vibrationally to this universal consciousness.

With this knowledge, we begin to understand and realize that we are more than what we see. Consider that you are more than your physical body, and without the essence or vibration of your spirit, the body is simply flesh. As you learn and experience physical existence, you develop your intellect and your consciousness which in turn shapes the development of your vibrational frequency—your spirit. As you further develop your consciousness, you allow yourself to return to your true form of spiritual energy. You become your full expression, your full potential as a spiritual being within your human existence. Understanding that you are more than just the standard physical definitions of "human" with one finite lifetime is the first step in the realization that you can climb the ladder of consciousness within you. During the development of your consciousness, on the way towards higher consciousness, enlightenment, or God, you begin to express your own divinity. What most people do not realize is that there are many levels past enlightenment, and that enlightenment is not the final destination or prize. The true path is finding yourself, the real you, who you were prior to entering your physical body. When you realize who you are and what you are, you can see how you are connected to everything, and that anything is possible in your physical and spiritual worlds.

Every experience you go through is one more step you take in unfolding the mystery of yourself. The more energy and effort you put into learning and studying spiritual teachings, the more you can apply them to your physical and spiritual development. This brings you one step closer to knowing your true self. With each life experience, you move closer to connecting to the higher self within your physical consciousness. When you achieve higher levels of consciousness, your human vibration increases and resonates to the level of your true capabilities and your purpose in life unfolds. As you increase your vibration, you increase your attraction and unfold your knowledge, experiences, and abilities effortlessly.

People who are able to express the consciousness of their higher vibrations lead amazing lives. Stephen Hawking was born on January 8, 1942 in Oxford, England, during the height of World War II. At an early age, Stephen was fascinated with learning and understanding how things worked. Stephen's father wanted him to study medicine at University College, Oxford, but Stephen was more interested in mathematics, which lead to his studies of physics. In his early twenties, Stephen went on to conduct research in cosmology at Cambridge. During the same time, he was diagnosed with Amyotrophic Lateral Sclerosis (ALS), also known as Lou Gehrig's disease, and was told by his doctor that he could possibly die within a few years. Initially distraught over the news of his incurable disease, Stephen went into momentary shock, but soon realized that there were people much worse off than himself. Stephen decided to continue his research and was soon engaged to Jane Wilde, whom he met around the time of his diagnosis. This relationship gave him even more reason to live. Even with his illness slowing him down, he finished his doctorate and continued his work in cosmology and theoretical physics.

In 1985, confined to a wheelchair due to ALS, Stephen caught severe pneumonia and had to have his trachea removed. This took away his ability to speak, but this problem was solved by a small portable computer and a speech synthesizer fitted to his wheelchair. Today, Stephen's work has helped explain the Big Bang theory, black holes and allowed him to postulate Hawking Radiation, a combination of quantum mechanics and the theory of relativity. Despite the struggles of his life experiences, Professor Hawking remains a great contributor in physics and has received many awards, medals, and prizes worldwide. He continues his research on theoretical physics and gives public lectures around the world.

Franklin Delano Roosevelt (FDR) was born in Hyde Park, N.Y., on Jan. 30, 1882. Graduating from Harvard after three years, he pursued a law degree at Columbia University and passed the bar examination in 1907. Roosevelt entered politics in 1910 and was elected to the New York State Senate as a Democrat. In 1913, he was appointed assistant secretary of the navy by President Woodrow Wilson. In 1920, he ran for vice president with James M. Cox, but they were defeated. Roosevelt returned to New York to practice law. In August, 1921, Roosevelt was stricken with infantile paralysis, also known as polio, and was left with partial use of his legs. Despite his physical disabilities, Roosevelt became governor of New York in 1928. In 1932, he received the Democratic nomination for president. During his unprecedented three full consecutive terms as the President of the United States, he brought hope to the nation by pulling the country out of the Great Economic Depression of the 1930s. Although he couldn't walk unassisted due to polio, Roosevelt ran the country during World War II. Franklin D. Roosevelt helped the American people find strength by regaining faith in themselves. He brought hope to the nation as he delivered a message of strength and encouragement in his Inaugural Address, "The only thing we have to fear is fear itself."

Oprah Winfrey was born on January 29, 1954, in Kosciusko, Mississippi. Oprah's parents were separated during her early childhood. She was sent to live with her grandparents in very poor surroundings until the age of 6 when she moved to live with her mother. While living with her mother, Oprah was sexually molested by male relatives into her teen years. By the age of 14, Oprah moved to Nashville to live with her father. His strict discipline taught her to make the best of her life, to not blame anyone but to seek strength within herself to overcome the hardships of her past. She entered Tennessee State University in 1971 at the age of 17 and began working in radio and television broadcasting in Nashville. By age 19, Oprah became the youngest and first African-American woman to anchor the news in Nashville, TN. By 1984, Oprah was recruited to host her own solo morning show, *A.M. Chicago*. Within a short period of time, Oprah's warm personal approach to television allowed her to surpass Phil Donahue in the ratings, putting her show in first place.

Soon, the *A.M. Chicago* took on the name of the *Oprah Winfrey Show*, and in 1986, became a nationally syndicated program. In 1988, she founded Harpo Productions, which soon gained ownership of her program from ABC. With nearly 50 million viewers in the U.S. and in 130+ countries internationally, the Oprah Winfrey show has remained the number one talk show for over two decades. She covers profound issues, raising awareness for poverty, illnesses, personal growth, along with many other topics. In April of 2000, Oprah and Hearst Magazine launched, *O: The Oprah Magazine* that now boasts a readership of over 2 million people. Forbes magazine reported that Oprah was the richest African American of the 20th century and hailed her as the most influential woman of her generation. Together with the Oprah Winfrey Foundation and the Oprah Angel Network, she has raised more than a hundred million dollars for global humanitarian efforts around the world. Oprah Winfrey came from a humble background to become one of America's most powerful and influential women in history.

These three individuals used the power within their own consciousness to overcome their hardships and realize their potential. What seemed like impossible physical and emotional setbacks were used by Professor Hawking, FDR, and Oprah as levers towards success and engagement with life because the issues were faced with strength and courage. They didn't rely on luck or willpower alone. Perhaps the source was their awareness of a greater purpose in life. Could it be that within the depths of their pain and suffering there lay a potent ability that allowed their experiences to unfold? As Winston Churchill superlatively said, "With great power comes great responsibility." The ability to allow your life to unfold begins with the awareness and belief of the unlimited potential that resides within us, regardless of beginnings, conditions, or perceived limitations.

When you understand your physical-spiritual makeup and the power of your vibrations that are associated with the levels of consciousness that exist within you, then you can allow everything to unfold within your life. The impossible becomes possible when you begin to recognize where you are in your own consciousness and spiritual evolvement; you realize the incredible and unique potential which awaits you. With any problem, addiction, or roadblock that you encounter in life, you must first recognize and identify that there is a problem. This acknowledgment shows you the boundaries of your mental thoughts. You first need to know where you are in order to get from point A to point B. In the same sense, you are able to understand what you need to accomplish and in which direction you need to go as you walk along your life's path. In the following chapters, we will discover the levels of consciousness within the human experience—the map of your physical and spiritual makeup on the road to enlightenment.

With the turning of the new millennium, we are standing at the doorstep of the second coming. This is the coming of our higher self, the expression of our spiritual potential, what the Mayan calendar refers to as the "Age of the Gods." When we understand and ascend past lower levels of consciousness in our physical bodies, we allow ourselves to be free from the negativity and mental boundaries of our illusionary world. We manifest our higher self, the potential of our spirit, to exist in our physical bodies. Never before have we been given the ability to perform such accomplishments, uniting our physical and spiritual self with greater ease and fluidity. To know your true self is to become one with your spirit. Conceptually, you no longer project your spirit into your physical body, but live within your spiritual and physical bodies united as one. This is the real meaning of becoming one with the universe. Living with our higher self allows us to live out our higher will, our higher purpose, for the good of the whole rather than living unaware and unconscious of ourselves, our environment, and our connection to each other.

Divine essence is selfless because it is a higher part of you. As you learn to accept yourself in your entirety, you are then able to freely accept others around you. When you are living at a higher level of consciousness, however you choose to map out your day will be of your choosing and no one else's. You take back control of your life. Just like when we are able to sense when someone is happy or angry, you can choose how you are affected by your emotions and how they will impact you. This is the law of cause and effect. You are a unique individual with your own ideas, your own life, and your own path. You create this according to where you are in your consciousness; the types of beliefs you have and the nature of your thoughts are the positive or negative attractions you project on an energetic level. What you choose, how you act and re-act, and what you do in your personal and professional life are expressions of who you are in your consciousness resonation. To choose to blame someone or something for your life circumstances dismisses who you are. You then become an expression of the consciousness of your environment and not your own expression.

Whether you have experienced heartache from losing someone you love, illness, separation or divorce, whether it is mental, physical or emotional pain or suffering that you go through, life's experiences invite you to challenge yourself to seek something more than what your present physical world has to offer. What has happened to your divine spirit since it was born into your current body? How have your experiences, social teachings, family relationships, personal and professional relationships, belief systems and environment colored the lens through which your spirit is seen?

Every day there are people from all walks of life, at different ages, from various countries, cultures and races that "awaken" and decide that they want to know what their existence means. What if there was a way to accelerate your spiritual growth or increase your connection with your truth? The person you were five years ago is different from the person you are today; the person you are today is different from the person you will be five years from now. What if you could learn more about the roadblocks in your personal life and figure out the steps you need to take in order to remove them and expedite your personal or spiritual growth? What if you could be shown how to accelerate through your karmic lessons and attract abundance, growth, fulfillment, and peace of mind into your life?

This book provides the information and answers to the struggles, issues, and questions that we all encounter in life. It will explain the progression and development of your physical and spiritual life through the human experience, the idea of karma, the various relationships within the self, and a preview of stages of enlightenment or awakening along the journey to finding your true self. Whether you choose to call it enlightenment, salvation, nirvana, or heaven, it is simply a path to finding the God within you. The way to do this is to discover where you are on your spiritual roadmap and measure where you are in your current life, and what you are attracting in your physical-spiritual consciousness. There have been many masters in the past who have shown a way that was appropriate for the understanding level of their time, but as a more advanced society, we need something that is appropriate for us today. What if you were shown your personal roadmap to enlightenment, so that you could jump start your spiritual development wherever you are in your present life? In the following chapters you will learn about your physical and spiritual development and how it unfolds within the human experience of your physical life. You will learn about the development of your spirit on its path to higher consciousness, and how you function within the physical existence. It all starts with *you*.

CHAPTER 2

SEEING A NEW LIGHT

November 2000, it was a cold and wet autumn that year. My mother, a recently committed Buddhist nun, was touring the U.S., helping the monks as they attended to a man considered to be "enlightened"—Zen Master Thich Thanh Thu. He was a kind, older gentleman, who was frail and gray at the age of 78. Although he walked with a cane, he had a bounce in his step and he exuded a sense of happiness and peace. His last stop on the lecture tour was in Seattle, WA. From there, he was to go back to Da Lat, Vietnam, to the temple where the master taught and resided. Because Master Thu was male, according to Buddhist etiquette, women were not allowed to attend to him. So, my brother and I were asked to escort him back to Vietnam. This also marked the first trip back to my homeland since fleeing the Vietnam War in 1975.

Although the plane ride was extremely long, I was excited to visit my birthplace. I would see my grandparents and relatives who helped take care of me when I was an infant, as well as a rebuilt country that had been torn apart by war. Because I was the eldest, I sat next to Master Thu during the twenty hour flight to Vietnam. Master Thu treated me as if I were his grandson, and I respected and cared for him as my elder. Being Christian at the time, I was curious about the whole "enlighten-ment" thing. I asked him several questions, to which I expected long, lengthy explanations. I asked, "What is enlightenment? What does it mean to be enlightened? What do you see when you are enlightened? How do you know you are enlightened?" Master Thu simply smiled at me and said, "Enlightenment is the Buddha nature found within all of us. It means to have love and compassion for all things and that our life is only a temporary illusion. When you are enlightened, you see yourself. You know you are enlightened, just like when you know how to ride a bicycle, you just know." He then smiled once again, took a sip of his herbal tea, and then drifted off to sleep. It was many years before I finally understood the power of his few simple words on the airplane ride. It was the same day that brought me back to the place where my life first began—Vietnam.

For most people the suggestion that "life is an illusion" conjures up feelings of confusion, denial, anger, and rejection. Misunderstanding often arises from hearing this short yet powerful statement. This may bring about questions such as, "What do you mean life isn't real? Are you saying I am not real? That my thoughts, feelings, and experiences are not real?" What if these responses are just defensive reactions that defend and embrace your life experiences to validate your identity? You assume that being human is real simply because you can see, smell, hear, taste, and touch. You validate the idea of being real through the emotional feelings of your experiences. If you think, talk, walk, sense, and feel, then why did the enlightened Buddha state, "Life is an illu-sion?" Does it only further spawn questions such as, "What is life? What is reality? What is illusion? What is enlightenment?"

If we break down the word *enlightenment,* phonetically it states *in the light we were meant.* Enlightenment is a state of being, existence, awareness, and a level of consciousness. We evolve into what we were before we came into our physical existence. We evolve from spirit, which is made up of a collective family of spiritual beings that energetically forms and creates the many levels, power, and force of consciousness that we know and feel inside of us. It's a part of each of us, connected to you as your spirit. This energy creates the unified force known to many as "God." At this state of consciousness, there is no separation, no judgment, no selfishness and no need for mass accumulation of wealth to validate or define the status of who we are in this world. Enlightenment is simply a state of unconditional love and acceptance in the awareness of all things.

The subject of enlightenment is not a new concept. For centuries, the state of enlightenment has been sought by millions and millions of people from all walks of life—Buddhists, Hindus, Christians, monks, nuns, scholars, men, women, and even children. More and more, people all over the world want to experience this state of being. Many of them have read books, scrolls, and spiritual teachings. They have attended sermons and classes, followed self-proclaimed masters and gurus. They have done countless hours of meditations, prayers, mantras, and yet not even a fraction of the world's population has achieved this state of being. Why? Because as the human race evolves, the older teachings and interpretations of enlightenment become outdated, misunderstood, and less relevant for us in our current context. As we advance, so must the ways and understanding of enlightenment advance in order for it to become more accessible to our time and our generation. The one thing that is true and will always remain true from our past and for many generations to come is that enlightenment is found within all of us. Enlightenment is available for all those who desire or allow themselves to obtain this level of consciousness.

When seeking to achieve enlightenment, or as Christianity would say, "salvation," we first need to redefine these terms in relation to today's level of understanding. In doing so we begin to lay down a foundation that is more concrete, definable, and achievable in relation to our society's more advanced intellect. When referring to God, I am not referencing a God of religion that is an all-knowing, omnipotent being who watches over me and decides whether or not I am going to heaven or going to hell. Instead, I refer to a God of universal creation and intelligence that is comprised of a multitude of different vibrations and frequencies. Within these frequencies exists the expansive creation of different energies, spirits, dimensions, and matter that makes up our universe as well as a multi-dimensional universe that we are now beginning to uncover in theoretical and quantum physics today. In spiritual form prior to our physical existence, you and I existed as a very high vibrating frequency that expresses spiritual energy within our physical body. In the union of our totality within universal consciousness, we are a part of the circle of light or the family that is God. This family includes everyone here on this Earth. When redefined in this light, we, in actuality, are God.

In striving to know God within you or achieving various levels of enlightenment, the difference between the people who have achieved this level of consciousness and those who are still striving is defined only within the mental boundaries that limit your spiritual potential. When you are able to free yourself of mental boundaries that limit what you can do or can't do, then you can learn to focus your energies to the level of intention, or vibration, to match that of your desire. You allow your spiritual energies to physically unfold through the human experience as your vibration rises to this state of being. Once this level of higher consciousness has been obtained, the whole knowledge of universal consciousness is opened up to you. Awareness dramatically changes your life. You no longer need to seek validation from the world around you. As Master Jesus said in John 8:23, "I am not of this world," when he himself obtained this level of higher consciousness.

Enlightenment, salvation, higher consciousness, or even God-consciousness are synonymous. This core concept has evolved with our human development. When we begin with an idea, depending upon how we view or perceive it within our consciousness, the original form begins to take on different meanings. Let us liken this to the evolution of the wheel. The wheel is seen everywhere today in various sizes, shapes, and forms. We see wheels on bikes, cars, trains, planes, machines, wagons, mechanical equipment, and countless other things. The wheel has become a necessity in our existence. But as important as the wheel is, nobody really knows who made the first wheel. The oldest wheel found in archeological excavations was discovered 3500 B.C. in Mesopotamia. Some archaeologists believe its origin to be in Asia around 8,000 B.C. Humans realized that heavy objects could be moved more easily if something round, such as a tree log, was placed under it and the object was rolled over it like a sled (or sledge). With time, the sledges started to wear grooves into the rollers that allowed objects to be carried further and faster. The log roller evolved into a wheel as humans cut away the wood between the two inner grooves to create what is now called an axle. With the axle and wheels creating all the movement, this lead to the creation of the first cart. As society and technology has advanced throughout the centuries, the wheel has evolved into countless variations. The original form of the wheel has not changed, but the uses and interpretations of the wheel have evolved.

The origin of human existence is similar to the evolution of the wheel. Throughout the centuries, the explanation of our origin has changed and evolved—starting with the worship of the earth and the sun, which evolved into Paganism, Buddhism, Hinduism, Islam, Judaism, Christianity, and so on. But as different cultures, countries, and societies have evolved, the origination of human existence has never changed. What we know to be true is that conception begins with the union of a male and a female. But just like the origin of the wheel, our beginning is still undetermined and unexplainable to the analytical mind. Some of us turn to various religions, spiritual teachings and science to help us explain the origin of existence. Each version of these teachings states an origin or explanation of our existence, but which one is right? The one thing we assume to be true, because it is consistent in most of these teachings, is that we will find out the truth in the afterlife. Until this takes place, the explanation of our origin as well as our afterlife has created variation and separation in our physical existence through the mental-emotional attachment of various scientific and spiritual teachings.

In society today, we see separation between these man-made versions of our origin and existence, which is fueled by the attachment of our own mental-emotional human pride. For thousands and thousands of years, society has tried to put together bits and pieces of our past with fossils and discoveries of scrolls, manuscripts, and books. The majority of these artifacts were destroyed as each new empire established their control throughout human history. We now have only incomplete historical artifacts from our past with modern versions of interpretation, which we have molded into religions, histories, and philosophies with varying degrees of consciousness. By holding onto the incomplete identity and emotional security of our past, we neglect our human potential within the present moment. As a species, we have created an intellectual and technological society. Just like the evolution of the wheel, we must evolve in our own understanding and consciousness that is appropriate for today's generation. Holding on to past ideas and interpretations of religions has only created pride, prejudice, separation, war and death.

As society advances, so must the ways and understanding so we may pave new ground to evolve consciously—not only for our society, but for our planet as well. The real path and purpose of everyone here on this planet is the path of understanding spiritual development through our physical experience in order to advance the growth of our spirit. Growth of the individual spirit directly and powerfully affects the consciousness growth of our population and our planet. The Dalai Lama states, "The whole purpose of religion is to facilitate love and compassion, patience, tolerance, humility, forgiveness." Mother Theresa stated, "If we have no peace, it is because we have forgotten that we belong to each other." Thich Nhat Hanh says, "Life can be found only in the present moment. The past is gone, the future is not yet here, and if we do not go back to ourselves in the present moment, we cannot be in touch with life." Within our present growth and development, we gain understanding and wisdom along the way to obtaining higher consciousness. This is simply a journey of returning back to who you were prior to coming into your physical life: a being of higher consciousness and pure light.

You may believe in re-incarnation. You may believe in a religion, whether it is Christianity, Buddhism, Taoism, Judaism, or simply an unidentified sense of spirituality or connectedness. What if there is no separation between religions, but only what you create in your own interpretation that limits your ability to obtain higher consciousness? Obtaining higher consciousness is not about what religion you follow or what you do or don't do in order to take that next step to get closer to God, Buddha, or simply a state of higher consciousness. Instead of trying to interpret the words of each individual religion, we should come to the realization that every religion or philosophy was introduced in a way that corresponded with the culture from which it originated and the period of its manifestation. A religion is inspired when you feel the vibration of God within yourself, from your higher self that is connected to this universal divine vibration. God, Buddha, or enlightenment is not found in a book or a set of scrolls. It is a vibrational presence felt within you, a state of being, a state of connectedness, and a state of higher consciousness. God cannot be fully understood or interpreted by the human mind, because God is not human. We, in our original form, are not human. We are spirit that exists momentarily in a human body and a human experience.

The core principles within all major religions are the same concepts repeated over and over again throughout the centuries. Emotional pride, judgments, and attachments to these man-made religions have created false interpretations. By empowering our lower consciousness, we create mental-emotional noise that causes us to lose our focus and bind us to lower level thinking. This is separation versus unification. Working out of our lower consciousness creates attachments to our self-created illusions. We are not living in awareness and acceptance. Everyone has their own purpose for being here with their own rate of growth in consciousness development. Without this understanding, we chase our emotions through belief systems that create the illusion of self righteousness and separation between individuals and nations. This separation was not the intention of our ascended masters.

When we view ourselves through the eyes of man-made religion and the relationship between "Man and God," we can see how it creates separation through human interpretation. This separation tells us that achieving "God" consciousness is not possible, that we are not worthy, we are sinners, and that we are simply not good enough.

Masters Jesus and Buddha helped raise the level of consciousness during their appointed time, several centuries apart from one another and in different parts of the world. The words are different, but the message is the same. The capability to reconnect ourselves back to God is within each and every one of us, especially now that we are a more evolved and advanced society. The key to finding the self is in knowing that you come from a divine vibration and intelligence, and not what man's prideful interpretations tell you. A truly enlightened master knows that there is no separation from you and the family of God. Separation only exists in man at his lower levels of consciousness.

Mental differences between religions cause separation within an already culturally fragmented society, manipulating us into chasing some unbalanced idealistic path to God or enlightenment. This limits our spiritual awakening. The older models of religions are based upon a model of rejection in order to achieve enlightenment or spiritual salvation. These older models are still used today in seeking the self. Based upon the present world's conscious state, it is too slow a process for the human population. Through the discoveries of science, frequency and the human vibration, there is now a much faster path to evolve our spiritual consciousness. You now have a choice that doesn't involve rejection of part or all that you are, but allows for understanding and acceptance of everything that you are.

Based upon what we now know from quantum mechanics, we have discovered that we are merely a collection of fast moving particles of vibrational matter, colliding against each other at a certain frequency to form what we can see with our eyes and touch with our hands. But just because we don't see something with our eyes doesn't mean that it doesn't exist. It means that the things that we don't see are simply vibrating at a much higher and faster frequency than we are capable of viewing with the human eye. When we get into our cars, turn on the radio to tune into our favorite radio station, out comes music and information. The reality is that radio frequencies exist all around us even though you and I cannot physically see or touch them. So, why can't there be things that exist whether we choose to believe in them or not? How about ghost, spirits, angels, even different dimensions? What you choose to believe in can either help or hinder your growth and development both physically and spiritually. This depends upon the way you mentally connect or attach to them. Ice melts into water and then evaporates into air. At each physical level, the molecular essence is the same, only the energetic expression is different.

Let's explore the explanation of creation through science. Within the last couple of decades, advances have lead scientists to decipher the structure of the atom. They have discovered a number of smaller particles. This has lead to a new study in theoretical physics, known as String Theory. String Theory states that frequencies are generated from enclosed vibrational loops, or strings, that resonate into particles.

These particles transmit forces to the particles that make up matter. This shapes the vibrating particles into a desired form, which then leads to infinite possibilities. Just like the vibration created from a guitar or violin resonate various notes of sound in order to create music, so are the strings that conform to the vibration of frequencies that create matter. Applying frequency at the human level, two cells (the egg and the sperm) come together to form an embryo. The embryo then multiplies and divides into a number of identical cells. Neurotransmitters, chemicals that modulate electrical signals (frequencies), are released and inputted into a group of cells that form the brain, then the spinal cord, organs, bones and muscles, until a fetus grows into a little baby inside the mother's womb.

When we look at the human nervous system and how it interacts with the body, we can begin to see how the human body works in terms of generating our human vibration, starting at the level of the atom. An atom is a particle charged by protons and neutrons and many smaller particles in between. These charged particles bang into each other to form mass, which takes on the various shapes of matter. If we look at the way our body and nervous system communicate, we see that our brain gives off electrical impulses that fire down our nervous system into our muscles or organs to communicate what we want our body to do. Our musculoskeletal system at the cellular level interacts with positive and negative charges to release chemicals that cause our muscles to create movement. Our bones have positive and negative charges that react to various stresses called the piezoelectric effect. Just about everything in your body produces electrical charges that interact with each other to generate your thoughts, memories, actions and emotions. Like satellites that transmit various radio frequencies from space, the human body emits the energies from thoughts and emotions through your spiritual body. Your spiritual body is an energy body that resonates energies, creating your aura. Understanding the laws of energy and attraction, you can consider how your daily interactions at a vibrational level allow you to attract or manifest the things that you want or don't want in your life. The power of your thoughts and emotions has a clear and definite impact on your physical body and what you draw to you or manifest in your life. As Dr. Bruce Lipton states in *The Biology of Belief*, "Our positive and negative beliefs not only impact our health, but also every aspect of our life."

Have you ever woken up one day in a terrible mood? Maybe you didn't get enough sleep the night before, or you woke up with a sharp neck or back ache. Maybe you simply woke up dreading getting out of bed because you hate your job. This heightened state of emotional restlessness can cause you to overreact to any sort of stimulation you may encounter, whether it's being stuck in morning rush hour, or spilling coffee on your shirt—everything seems irritating to you. The opposite response is to numb yourself to your surroundings, causing you to check out emotionally. You may forget to grab your important documents for a meeting that day, or arrive to work late—nothing seems to matter. How you act and react to your emotional attachments defines your perceptions and how you interact in your daily life. When you can recognize how you attach to your thoughts and emotions, you can rewrite the mental programs of your emotional energies and free yourself from negative attraction.

We, as a collective spiritual energy, created our physical existence in order for the spirit to learn and experience the whole of creation. Before you entered your physical body, you were part of universal consciousness. When you leave this physical life, you are absorbed back into this consciousness to be utilized in other ways that are deemed necessary to continue the balance and creation of all things. The physical life experience, in relation to the spirit, is crucial for your spiritual connection, development, and continued existence. It represents the reason for creation. The growth and development of the spirit through the physical experience leads you back to the origin of your connection. It is the vibration of universal consciousness. In other words, you learn and experience the many levels of your spiritual makeup through your physical life. Life is an illusion, a program that you create in order to learn and grow your spirit.

You see the conditioning of this program all around you. If you don't drive a fancy car, have a big house or have a nice job that makes you lots of money, then you haven't "made it." If you don't look like this person or act like that person, have not achieved what another person has achieved, then you are "not good enough." If you don't have an education or a graduate degree then you must not be "smart enough." When you realize that these false validations are self-created by your own illusions, that you are attached to them and empower them with your mental thoughts and emotions, you can see how you program your mind with these falsehoods. These are lies that you tell yourself. When you no longer need the world's validation, then you are no longer of this world. Master Jesus said of himself in John 8:23, "You are from below; I am from above. You are of this world; I am not of this world." This awareness allows you to break free from your mental attachments and society's program in your lower levels of consciousness. The world you view as the place of constant struggle to succeed and achieve is preoccupied with the false validation of others.

Just as one brick that stands alone remains a brick, many bricks placed together in the perfect order create the temple that houses the people within it. You are part of the foundation of the temple, an integral part that supports and provides strength to its structure. You are part of the family, and the family makes up the whole. Without the family, you are only a small piece of the structure, which is why you may perceive yourself to be separate from the family of God. You don't realize the importance of the brick that is part of the temple. As an individual spiritual being, you make up a part of a whole vibration and every part of this vibration has its purpose. Without mortar and structure, we would be a bunch of bricks in disarray without a purpose. Without structure, we may crumble with the slightest touch or movement within our surroundings, and within the world. As a unique spiritual being, you have your purpose in the genetic makeup of universal consciousness (light versus dark) which gives rise to balance, structure, and flow. Being part of your divine vibration is to know that you have a spiritual connection to your higher self. When you come to the realization that there is no separation between man and God, that you are of God and as a whole are God, then you can ascend the ladder of consciousness. This allows you to not only raise consciousness within you, but also to access your spiritual gifts, to access and control your spiritual body. When you empower and attach to things that are outside of you, you lessen your spiritual vibration and give away the power and the strength of your vibration.

Consciousness starts with understanding the basic principles of creation and the origins of the human vibration. Based upon scientific evidence today, we can look at spiritual development from the origins of vibration in relation to the human experience. This helps us understand the older models of obtaining enlightenment and get us there faster. If we look at creation in terms of vibration, we created the spirit to exist as a fragment of the whole vibration. This allows the spirit to understand creation and all that it has to offer by experiencing spiritual growth through physical existence.

We created the spirit in order to experience the self. We learn and grow through the experience of the illusion of our attachments to the daily programs that we create. This is an important concept that supports the paradigm shift taking place. We are spiritual beings in a physical experience. The old paradigm of religion states we are physical beings longing for a spiritual experience or connection when we seek God or enlightenment. As Dr. William A. Tiller states in *Science and the Human Transformation*, "...we are spirits having a physical existence." Non-physical entities such as spirits, angels, ghost, or demons are resonating spiritual energies that exist at a higher, faster vibration that is not visible to the human eye. Who you were before your physical existence is spiritual energy—a higher vibrational frequency. Therefore, your true spirit form is a higher vibrational frequency that cannot fully exist within the lower vibrational frequency of the physical body. Your spirit diffuses its frequency by projecting itself into the physical body in order to have the physical experience. Your physical form is your spirit's lowest, most dense frequency. As spirit, you project yourself downward or separate your higher vibration into lower frequencies to exist within the physical body. In doing so, you are able to lower the vibrational frequency of your spirit so that it can exist within your physical body and live out the physical experience. In this projection or separation of the spirit, we can also explain the existence of past lives and karma in your spiritual genetic makeup which makes up the first seven chakra bodies of the spirit. At higher enlightened states of consciousness, you raise your spiritual vibration and remain fully connected to universal consciousness.

There are many ways to describe and approach your spiritual development. Just like how we can view and describe the human body from its visual appearance of front, side, back, color, shape, and size that define our outward physical expressions. We can also describe the human body from its internal physiological infrastructure, such as the nervous system, organ system, vascular system, and so on. The first seven chakras, situated vertically along the spine up through the crown of the head, represent one way of looking at the spirit's internal genetic infrastructure. The chakra system holds fragments of your spiritual identity within the vibrational frequency of each energy center.

The first seven chakra bodies of the lower self (your physical self) show a path of development and the path of consciousness within the self. These are studied in Buddhism, yoga, and other Eastern religions. Through science and the human vibration, there arises an advanced correlation to the older models of religion and consciousness evolvement. Understanding the ways and concepts of the past through our current knowledge and understanding expedites our spiritual growth toward higher consciousness. Before you place your efforts on raising your energies, you must understand the structure of the temple that houses your spiritual energies. Your body is a vessel that contains the roadmap for your journey towards enlightenment and the higher vibrations of higher consciousness.

CHAKRAS

CHAPTER 3

CHAKRAS

The word *chakra* originates from Sanskrit meaning wheel or disk. Chakras are bio-energetic centers of informational energy that resonate, assimilate, and express various stages of physical and spiritual existence. They pertain to levels of consciousness, developmental stages of life, archetypes, elements, colors, sounds, and body functions. The chakra system consists of seven main lower energy centers that extend from the base of your spine to the top of your head. Depending upon which chakra level you are accessing, you unfold the energetic information held within the chakra's energy vortex. This is energy that is being exchanged within the magnetic field of your environment. They allow you to create, attract, manifest and experience the information and lessons that each chakra holds as your spiritual growth unfolds. In essence, a chakra is a revolving vortex of energy that can flow in two directions, inward or outward, receiving or providing energetic information between your spirit and your physical existence.

Chakras function in a similar way to the nervous system. Energetic nerve impulses run back and forth through your nervous system to communicate information from your brain to various parts of your body. The energetic information that is continually exchanged communicates the overall status and function of your physical body. In order for your body to function well, the energetic nerve impulses must communicate information to your muscles and organs supporting your arterial, venous, lymph, and hormonal systems. This information orchestrates the proper functions for digestion, assimilation, movement, and circulation. Similarly, the seven lower chakras that exist within the physical body create your core spiritual energy center. On a bio-energetic level, each chakra center relays the information of your spirit through the creation of the energy body. The energy or spiritual body resonates, assimilates, and expresses itself energetically to the magnetic energy field of your environment, thus uniting your energy body to the energy field all around you to create union and integration that is continuous with universal consciousness and creation. The creation of the energy body is extremely vast and complex. Together, the seven major lower chakra centers, the meridian system used in acupuncture, and the minor chakra centers located in various areas within the body create the resonation field of the entire energy body, which is perceived as your aura.

When unified, opened, and balanced, the seven lower chakras express the power, wisdom, and expression of universal consciousness, or your spirit. When unbalanced, the consciousness held within each energetic chakra center magnifies its expression, which creates separation and exaggerated expression of your spiritual fragments. Just as one string plucked from a guitar makes one clear sound, multiple strings plucked at random create disharmony and noise. When played in unison and in perfect order, you create beautiful music that can express many powerful meanings and emotions felt within a song. Understanding the purpose for each chakra and how it correlates within the development of your physical and spiritual consciousness allows you to know and understand where you are in your own consciousness development. As the understanding of the chakras has evolved with the evolution of Earth's population, it is now being applied to traditional and modern spiritual teachings, including yoga, and Eastern and energy medicine.

In the next seven chapters, we will explore the chakras from a new vantage point. We will look at the correlation of the chakras to advanced sciences, the human vibration, and the connection to consciousness development within the physical existence. You can think of your chakras as discs of stored information of your spirit and its multitude of past life experiences and karma. Your chakras hold the different parts of your spiritual experience which is accessed as your consciousness development increases and unfolds within your physical existence.

Within the human experience, your ability to see, touch, hear, taste, and smell are the receptors that create your thoughts, perceptions, and emotions. These are the building blocks of chakras one through four that transition and develop the spirit within the physical existence. The fourth through seventh chakras help develop and integrate your spirit into your physical existence. The fourth chakra body, your heart chakra, bridges the integration of your energetic spiritual body to your physical existence. The heart chakra begins to express the energetic power of your feelings and emotions. This is the power of your spiritual energy that creates real purpose and meaning in your life. Your heart chakra contains the reason why your spirit came to learn from your life experiences. It contains your spirit's soul. Whether you are in balance or not, you resonate the experiences of your spiritual consciousness by attracting the many different experiences you encounter in life, allowing you to experience more of who you are.

When your life experiences seem too challenging for you to handle—whether you lose your job, suffer heartache from a failed relationship, the death of a loved one, or go through the experience of having someone you trust lie to you—these experiences may get the best of you. In letting your emotions consume you, you create attachment to the experience. This is the mental-emotional development of the spirit within the first four chakras. These chakras teach you to learn and master your emotional identity in your physical existence, through your mental-emotional attachments. An emotional spike in your mental-emotional energies can throw your energy field out of alignment, which means that your chakras are not in balance. You then experience the associated negativities around emotion, similar to when a music CD skips and repeats itself when it is scratched. You become annoyed.

As you grow older, you gain more life experiences. The things that seemed to once push your buttons or drive you to want, desire, or control add a little less juice to your emotions as you mature. How you respond to your first relationship, first love, first marriage, or first child is probably a lot different than after a few relationships, a few marriages, and a couple of children. Your first job is probably completely different from the job you have today. When you move from a basic existence of survival, identity, accumulation, and attention to a higher plane of sharing, empowering, respecting, and loving what you already have, you begin to realize that making time for yourself becomes more important than making money. Spending more time with your kids or a loved one becomes more important. Why? As you ascend the ladder of your consciousness, you begin to be inspired by the development of who you are in spirit.

In understanding your consciousness development in the context of your physical existence, you can learn to recognize where and when you are balanced or imbalanced by the way you attach to your life experiences. Being exposed to and learning from your experiences, negative and positive, will help you grow faster and allow you to experience more of who you are within the spiritual energies of the chakra bodies. As you ascend your levels of consciousness, you accelerate your spiritual growth and development. For the purpose of this book, we will focus on the seven lower chakra centers of the spirit. The first seven chakra bodies hold the information of your spiritual roadmap to unfolding your physical life and ultimately, evolving your spirit. Finding out where you are on your own personal roadmap of spiritual consciousness helps you recognize, balance, and accelerate your spiritual growth, making it possible to reach levels of enlightenment within your lifetime.

CHAPTER 4

ROOT
CHAKRA

The first chakra body, also known as the root charka, is located at the base of the spine. It represents your human connection to Mother Earth as it grounds your spirit to your physical existence. It is the womb from which life is birthed for the existence of all species. It represents your spirit's transition into physical form. It is your spirit's orientation to self-preservation through the animal instinct of survival, and the security of human survival within the physical existence. It is the transitional vortex for the spirit as it projects into the physical body in preparation for your existence in the physical plane. Your spirit roots itself to the physical body through the first chakra. Just as the physical body grounds itself to the Earth, the root chakra provides the means to ground your spirit to your human existence.

Within the basic foundation of life, we share the same survival needs with all species. Generation after generation, various living organisms and species continually evolve to ensure their longevity and survival. This best explains the expression of the first chakra body, the first level of consciousness, the need for the continuation of your own survival. The first chakra provides you with your physical expression and acts as a reminder that life existence can be as simple as your basic needs to eat, sleep and procreate. This first level of consciousness manifests your animalistic instinct to survive first and foremost. Without it, no living species would be able to thrive.

If we look at human survival in a modern day sense, most of us live our lives focused on what we don't have and what we are willing to do in order to get what we "believe" we need as a means of survival. The act of survival in today's society is no longer focused on the basic necessities of existence, but the things and objects that we perceive we "lack" in order to validate our lives or make them better. The act of accumulation, whether it is making money, buying nice cars, eating at expensive restaurants, or living in a big house, provides us with a sense of social identity and security. It makes us temporarily believe that we have succeeded in our lives. It creates an illusion of security within our physical life.

But after we achieve our goals, we begin to set new goals. We continually strive for our own self improvement. This then feeds our animalistic instinct of domination and control as a means to socially survive. We commonly do this through acquiring material excess while seeking and attaching to excitement, pleasure, and convenience for the conscious mind. We work through the "middle self" (our physical self) in order to feel a greater sense of ease in our environment. How much do you need to feel complete? What kinds of things or experiences are needed to validate who you are? What are you identifying with that provides you the mental happiness you seek? You begin your human and spirit integration through the process of experiencing your physical life. Trial and error takes you through the development of your attachments, judgments, and aversions within your experience in order to measure and create your physical and mental development. This is your perceptual human instinct of survival. As your life progresses, you continually learn about and evolve your spiritual growth through the intellect and wisdom of the human experience.

The middle self is a metaphysical term that represents the conscious human part of your spirit. Your middle self processes all the energetic information gathered from your learning experiences. You learn by acquiring knowledge through the human experience—the everyday events, actions, emotions, encounters, and choices that you make along the way. Your knowledge, perspective, and understanding of each experience is usually directed by the level of your consciousness development in relation to the self and its energetic relation to your environment. This allows you to attract and manifest your life experiences. In other words, the way that you receive and react to your experience is dictated by your experience, knowledge, and wisdom at the level of your current level of consciousness. It is all relative to your awareness, similar to how a person who knows how to swim may view the ocean differently than one who is afraid of water. Water exists with or without us. It is there for our experience to unfold and does not change in its existence in any way, shape or form. It is our individual perspectives and how we mentally and emotionally attach to water that creates different understandings and relationships with it.

In our initial learning process, the majority of us are often driven by the emotional attachments of the misunderstood "ego." Misunderstanding the ego rises from not understanding the development of your spirit within your physical existence. The projection of your spirit from universal consciousness into the physical body creates your seven chakra bodies, the spiritual energy center or fragments of your lower self. This allows you to unfold the development of your spirit and integrate its knowledge during your human development. As you experience life by attaching to the energy field of the environment, you allow the experience to dictate, satisfy, and develop your mental-emotional needs and desires.

From there, you form the foundations of your "emotional body." The emotions that direct your perceptions, judgments, and attachments are felt, created, and realized in a manner similar to when you are moved by a story from a good book or movie. Fear, the adrenaline felt after witnessing an abusive act, the pain felt when witnessing the loss of someone that you cherish, these exposures generate the energetic emotions that you witness through your human senses.

Initially, the spirit projects itself into the body like a beam of light is projected from a flashlight. An infant is more directly connected to spirit energetically and perceives information from the environment vibrationally. As the neural senses of the nervous system develop within the body, your spirit pulls and separates its energy as it directs its energy into the different chakra bodies (energy centers) and meridian channels to form your energy body that coexists within the physical body. The energy body directs the life force of your spirit through your chakras and meridian channels that together create the flow of human energy (chi). Your spirit's energy then becomes fragmented into the chakras in ascending order. The root chakra then becomes the spirit's entry point into physical existence.

As you grow and evolve as a human being, you begin the integration of the subconscious into the conscious. The subconscious begins to battle for acknowledgment and identity within the physical self. As your intellect develops, you create various likes and dislikes that your brain then categorizes by importance. This in turn fuels the struggle of your mental identity and its importance within the self, created by what is perceived as needed for survival. The subconscious mind's need for survival initially is ruled by the power of your emotions versus the intellect of the conscious mind. This separation fuels the false belief that you need to be in control of yourself and your environment, and the need to feel superior or dominant. This is a natural part of the animalistic instinct for survival. It can cause separation not only within you, but also from those around you. The thought process and actions at this first level of consciousness in your root chakra grounds you to your basic primal, and sometimes carnal instincts, known as your *animalistic ego.*

Dr. Carl Jung describes the lower levels of consciousness in stages. The initial entry levels of human development and the forming of your consciousness are often referred to as the development of the internal "athlete" or "warrior." The need for attention and self preservation is the initial driving force of your mental existence. It motivates you to want a sense of dominance or superiority within your surroundings. At the consciousness level of most people, there is no attachment to the emotionally undeveloped ego. There only exists the animal nature that creates the basic need for survival and security within your surroundings. In the animal nature, a function evolves within the community that is developed out of the masculine and feminine roles and energies: animalistic nature and nurture. Animalistic nature is the protective instinct of survival, and nurture provides for the supportive instinct of survival.

In your human need to have the animalistic ego coincide with the development of the self within its surroundings, you self-create and attach to illusions of the mind through your different levels of consciousness and understanding. This initially helps you to learn and define your growth within the perception of your judgmental duality of "good" versus "bad," "light" versus "dark." The conditioning of your social views and consciousness forms your beliefs and value systems within your conscious mind. The question remains: are your judgments, values, and beliefs true for you based upon your limited exposure or are they a result of your mental programming, social conditioning or the media's current focus or world view?

The idea of smoking tobacco has been conditioned to be viewed as unhealthy, but Indian tribes used smoking tobacco for spiritual healing and cleansing rituals for centuries. Alcohol ingested in excess dulls our mind and our senses, but is used as mediums for increased body absorptions of medicinal herbs in Chinese medicine. The exposure to a potentially harmful virus is considered to be unhealthy, but millions of people around the world receive flu vaccinations, a weakened flu virus strain, to help create antibodies in preparation of the human body's defense against getting sick with the flu.

Through reinforced mental conditioning at your lower levels of consciousness, you create false perceptions and judgments that filter into your experiences through your thoughts, emotions, and actions. This brings about a false interpretation of the "ego." The ego is an essential part of you and your consciousness development. Society, religion and philosophy have conditioned us to believe that the ego is a bad thing and that we must reject it. Your ego is the evolving sub-consciousness of your "inner child," usually left behind in the transition and development of the conscious or "middle self" when you reach early adulthood. When the ego is underdeveloped, you begin to nurture a sense of lack, fear, or insecurity through the need to be soothed, recognized or desired. This evolves from the spiritual neglect or separation of the inner child (subconscious) with the middle self (conscious). This separation heightens the lack of self worth, of feeling unfulfilled within the world of the conscious self amongst your peers and in your environment.

Everything in existence needs a good support structure and time in order to evolve into its full expression or true being. A seed needs time to grow with the help of the soil, water, sun, and favorable conditions of its environment. A car or piece of machinery needs people to make its parts and then assemble them before it can become fully functional for our use. A child needs the proper nurturing and support from their parents, friends, and social surroundings to help him or her develop into a healthy, active, and functional adult. Similarly, every aspect of your spiritual development takes time to grow into its full expression. The inner child, ego, middle self, higher self, and chakra fragments work in unison to create the full expression of your spirit.

The rejection or denial of any one of these parts stalls your evolvement and creates malfunction or incompleteness within your spiritual progression and potential. The core essence of survival is found within your existence which supports life. Your emotional boundaries and attachments to your mental perceptions create the development of the experience, which then creates your animal instinct of survival in the animal nature of existence.

What has happened when an individual expresses hatred, cruelty, savagery, or any of the dark sides of humanity? When deeply rejected in a negative expression, the ego can give way to the representation of what Carl Jung describes as the "shadow." This is the darkest part of us that enables our potential for human cruelty, whether directed at ourselves or towards others. This heightened state of an individual's pure expression of selfishness represents what is often referred to as the "me" mentality: what can I do for myself to gain control or dominance within my environment? These dark expressions occur when the root chakra is severely blocked or unbalanced, causing heightened emotional neediness.

On the other hand, the same vibration of the root chakra empowered in a positive manner is the force that drives our ambitions or desires to better ourselves or succeed within the environment. It is what separates one person from another when they harness their energies either positively or negatively. We express these attributes in much of our decision making and actions on a daily basis, through our interactions with other people. In essence, the ego is an energetic expression that when stimulated directs your emotional needs. Employed in either a positive or negative direction, the ego is a mirror of your inner sub-conscious expression of what you still haven't accepted as part of your own possible expression. At a motivational or emotional level, the need for survival, domination, or superiority comes forth to be acknowledged consciously by the "middle self." We are all capable of greatness or maliciousness based upon our own self-nurtured state.

We are stimulated by the animal nature within. The way we choose to vibrationally attach to a person or an environment gives rise to our outward animalistic expression.

What's the difference between a good person and a bad person? What's the difference between a powerful person and a greedy person? What's the difference between a narcissistic person and a person that is extremely insecure? There is no difference. It's the way we attach to our perception of a person that defines these labels. In essence, we are all capable of committing all sorts of acts, whether they are perceived or labeled as morally good or bad. Labels of good and bad are formed by your perceptions and judgments, which constantly evolve and change based on your perspective or level of consciousness. The freedom to be able to choose how you perceive, attach, or react to the events to which you expose yourself and to determine what is good or bad, is the experience of your "free will."

During your youth, the initial evolvement of your consciousness only knew and understood a limited measure of your perceptions that were enforced by your conditioned learning and by your experiences. As you gain more and more exposure through learning, you change and gravitate to more knowledge within your experiences, allowing for more understanding and less judgment. Eventually, this will allow you to evolve mentally and spiritually as your consciousness increases and draws more from your understanding rather than your emotions. We tend to focus our emotional energies in the direction that best supports our perception or judgment, based upon the consciousness level and understanding within the self. The goal is to raise your vibration equally through all of the levels of consciousness, allowing you to remove the feeling of lack or separation within yourself. You recognize and unify the fragments of the spirit's various identities or expressions that form the development and personality of your ego. When this is achieved, it allows you to be fully conscious within your physical body. You can then live your full spiritual potential within your physical existence. In doing so, this allows you to feel vibrationally connected to everything you see, feel, and sense around you. You vibrationally attract to you what is yours through the synchronicity of your own physical-spiritual resonation.

Within the development of the first chakra, the sense of survival remains a part of your consciousness until you are able to evolve that consciousness enough to let go of the need to control your environment. Struggling to survive in the world beyond your basic physical needs constantly reinforces a need to validate yourself. You relate survival to your need for acquiring more and more excess. Whether wealth or material consumption is used to define your identity in the world, this in essence displays to the world a sense of "lack" within yourself. When you chase after your immediate desires, you pursue the emotional need for instant gratification mentally, emotionally, sexually, physically, or materially. The mere act of following your emotions is sometimes as simple as determining that what you see is what you like, and that's all there is to it. Chasing emotional gratification can drive your animalistic, carnal desires to create a need of false dependency. Within the creation of your physiological emotions, you set forth the birth of your "emotional body" or the opening of the second chakra body.

Recognizing where you are in your outlook toward life allows you to understand and be aware of who you are at any present moment; you function with what you have until you can move on to the next level of awareness and understanding. When you function at the level of the animalistic ego, you may realize that your fear in reference to physical, material, or social survival gets in the way of your consciousness. Does this serve a purpose? It does if you were to only exist at survivalist consciousness. Keeping your eyes on the prize motivates and helps you to achieve personal wants, needs or goals in your life. This foundation is rooted in the level of thought that says, "If I do this, then I will get that." The basic expression of human exchange at lower levels of consciousness is motivated by fears that are rooted within survival instinct. At this level, you create mental rationalizations or justifications, such as lying, stealing, or harming others in order to acquire something that you feel you need or deserve. To move past the fear of being vulnerable, transparent, and not achieving the things you want is to let go of the fear of lack, result, and consequence; thereby allowing for the vibration of who you are to attract and manifest in your life versus you trying to force and control it.

The perceived balance between good or bad, light or dark within the human consciousness has a dual effect on your thoughts and actions, depending on how you choose to empower those thoughts. The power of your thoughts and intentions emit the positive or negative energetic vibration that attracts and creates the illusions that you mentally perceive. These energies not only have an effect on you, but also affect everyone and everything that you encounter within the energy field of your surroundings. The majority of our population lives their lives motivated out of fear at lower levels of human consciousness. The emotion of fear is what drives the force behind the survival instincts within you. To become exposed is to become vulnerable to the outside world; however, within the vulnerability comes empowerment of the self to become something greater, to attain spiritual consciousness.

The key is to understand that you are much greater than your physical existence. This recognition leads you to become vulnerable or open to your spirit. You are more than your physical body and your physical life. When you understand your true self, then you can empower yourself and understand how to grow and develop without mental boundaries. When you know you are more than your physical self, then you can move past the illusion of the mental mind to the next level of understanding and the next step along the roadmap of consciousness.

Simply put, you must look at the "ego" as a reflection or reminder of your current state of consciousness and a necessary expression in your life. If you take this into consideration, then you can see that all living things exist with animalistic ego tendencies. From a single cell protozoan to a complex human being, all life exists for survival. Before the human mind came into consciousness, we existed just like all other living species. We took in food to digest it for fuel and survival. We lived for basic needs that enabled existence. As we evolved and added our self-generated thoughts from the human intellect, we then reflected our level of understanding back to ourselves through the physical experience. The voice of the ego reflects our mental dialogue in order to keep us aware of where we are in our spiritual growth. It is a "checks and balances" system for our mental and spiritual consciousness.

As our species evolved the spiritual intellect, we modified our basic functions into urges and desires. Like the animal nature from which we originated, we have labeled our former reality with selection. Our desire to function is now redirected to our desire to dominate as a means of social survival. Just like the animal that needs to feed, humans have created the need to dominate, accumulate, and achieve superiority in a global consciousness that supports social survival.

Beyond our basic physical needs, we've created the need to have better pay, better jobs, nicer cars, bigger houses, so on, and so on. Is it really necessary to want to drive a car that is worth half a million dollars versus ten thousand dollars? Is it better to go from 0-60 mph in 4.5 seconds versus 15 seconds? Does driving an expensive car, say a Bentley, Ferrari, or Porsche make you feel more important than driving a Ford, Chevy, or Honda? Would you care more about the damage to your car, or the physical pain that you or the person feels after being involved in a motor vehicle accident? Society's perception of survival within the illusion of success has misconstrued the reality of existence, and hence the falseness of our needs that create our mental attitude toward social survival. Desire has now become the driving force and replaces our basic survival with more complicated "needs." To know your own desires is to understand how the body and brain work in conjunction with one another. To have this animalistic ego concept that exists within all of us is to understand where we come from, starting from ancient histories of empires forged from the power of an animalistic ego.

When we look back at world history, we see that most great empires rose from the domination of a survivalist mentality, evoked by the conscious realm of the animalistic ego. Alexander the Great, king of Macedon (336–323 BC), was one of the most victorious Greek military commanders in all of history. By the time of his death, he had conquered most of the known world. During his reign, Alexander conquered the Persian Empire and extended Mesopotamia's boundaries as far as the Punjab. He had planned to conquer Europe, and plotted to march eastward in order to find what he believed to be the end of the world. His childhood tutor, Aristotle, had related tales about where the land ends and where the Great Outer Sea begins. Alexander's dreams of domination were ended by his early death at the age of 33. His conquests ushered in centuries of Greek settlement and cultural influence over distant lands This was the period known as the Hellenistic Age, in which Greek and Middle Eastern culture were combined. Alexander's fame lives on in Greek history and mythology.

Gaius Julius Caesar (100/102–44 BC) is one of the most influential individuals in classic antiquity. His rule transformed the Roman Republic into the Roman Empire. By conquering Gaul, he extended the Roman reach all the way to the Atlantic Ocean. After gaining control of the Roman government, Caesar implemented far reaching reforms throughout Roman society and government. He centralized the Republican bureaucracy and assumed the roles of ruler and dictator. His dominating power ultimately led to his assassination, which was plotted by Marcus Brutus along with other conspiring senators. Unfortunately, their actions only ignited another Roman civil war, and eventually led to the establishment of the autocratic Roman Empire by Caesar's adopted heir, Augustus. Two years after his assignation, the Roman Senate officially sanctified Julius Caesar as a Roman deity. Caesar's fame lives on today, celebrated in countless movies and books. His military campaigns and rule, which were captured in his writings, speeches, and poetry, have been studied by historians and students throughout the centuries.

Born as Temüjin from the Borjigin clan, Genghis Khan (1162–1227 AD) went on to unite the Mongol tribes and founded the Mongol Empire—the largest contiguous empire in world history. Although he is a beloved figure in Mongolia, known as the father of the Mongol Nation, Genghis Khan is also remembered for his ruthless and bloodthirsty conquests. He formed the Mongol Empire through elimination of nomadic tribes of Northeast and Central Asia, purging ethnicities and consolidating land as he went along. He invaded Western Xia during the Jin Dynasty in northern China, as well as the Khwarezmid Empire in Persia. His immense reach covered most of Asia and Eastern Europe. The power of his empire lasted for more than 150 years after his death.

Was there a purpose for this kind of brutal activity within our human evolution? On a grand scale, within the process of domination through conquering and unionizing various nations, the integration of knowledge, beauty, and wisdom that each separate nation had to offer was forged. This allowed for each nation to learn from the other through the merging of disparate cultures. Knowledge within each nation created a conglomerate of the previous identities. Could this same effect have been achieved through more peaceful means? Most likely not, if you consider the level of consciousness at the time of these rulers.

Through your own desires to advance and achieve different things in your life, you use the power of the animalistic ego to attract others to support the direction of your consciousness and beliefs. Such an ability to create is possible for individuals and the greater collective. The creation of empires exists in modern times through large corporations, social groups, charities, communities, and even religious groups. This creates a single force of collective consciousness that can control the desire, direction, and intentions of a group. When you understand the power that the ego can exert through your emotions, you can see that if used in the right manner, with the right energetic intention, the ego can promote immense goodwill. So when you really know the ego for what it is, you can combine it with the conscious intellect of your higher self and draw forth the highest expression of the self.

As you develop, you may come to realize that you are returning to the spiritual vibration of your higher self. When you come to full realization of who you are, where you've been, and what you've experienced in life, you can see that you are an expression of your spiritual vibration. Depending on the level of consciousness at which you resonate as you grow, you can see a correlation between the lessons in life that you are exposed to and the karmic debt that is attached to the spirit at every level of consciousness resonation. The karmic lessons you are exposed to are the vibrational memories imprinted within your spiritual makeup that remain unresolved from past lives. These vibrational memories manifest outwardly through the lessons gleaned from your attachments. Experiencing these lessons within your physical life, then accepting and moving past them, are required in order for resolution of your spirit. Acceptance within yourself helps to advance your spiritual growth, which adds to the dimensions of your spirit. Who you are and how you perceive is a reflection of the level of consciousness at which you resonate. Your level of consciousness determines your judgments and your beliefs. Your perceptions dictate how you live your life, remain stuck, or advance in your spiritual growth. You dictate your life based upon the level of your consciousness; your human vibration determines the level at which you can comprehend life and your own purpose in the world, both physically and spiritually.

Buddhism teaches that "You are not your mind and your thoughts are meaningless." If you had no thoughts to implement, then your mind and body would continue to function on their own for your spirit's existence and your physical survival. When you add in your thoughts, then you sway your existence toward a certain direction based on your perceptions, judgments, and attachments. These are based purely upon your conditioned individually biased paradigms, based on the way you were raised, socialized, and educated. Through a collective energy in the form of thoughts, emotions, actions and reactions in your life, you generate and create your human vibration.

Knowing about the role of your carnal functions and the development of your false needs helps you to understand the development of the human spirit and how it pertains to your experiences in life. When you feel like you have reached your lowest point, it is your animalistic ego that fuels your desire to pick yourself up and pushes you forward in order to survive. The survival instinct of the human spirit is a very powerful and useful function. It is where a father finds the strength to lift a massive rock off the body of his child, or where a marathon runner pushes her body past its limits in order to seize a victory.

What the animalistic instinct truly represents is the desired outcome and the focus on what matters most to an individual at that present moment. The animalistic instinct provides for the level of focused energy within a desired want or need. Your first level of consciousness involves the survival or animalistic instinct that drives you to exist on a daily basis. When you live in your first level of consciousness, you live life based on your need for survival. At this level, there is a dichotomy of existence: one that is biased and one that isn't. Your thoughts and perceptions dictate your bias, usually one that is self-serving. This then becomes the force behind actions that drive the spirit depending on what the ego is focused on, which are usually desires motivated by lack or fear. When you desire selfishly, you strive for your own personal advancement. Are the things that you do for yourself based on your fear of social survival? Ask yourself, "What do I really need, and what do I really want in order to acquire or achieve something for my personal advancement?"

If we look at the dynamic structure of money, our attachment to money changes as we change our perception in relation to our lives. To a child, a hundred dollar bill would seem to be an enormous amount of money. It can be used to buy lots of candies and toys. This is a carnal pleasure that kids enjoy everywhere in the world. To an adult, depending upon a person's income bracket, spending a hundred dollars or losing it could be a significant or insignificant matter. A person who makes minimum wage, and has a child to take care of, feed, and clothe while paying for living and housing expenses—to this person, a hundred dollars can mean a lot. To a person who makes a few hundred thousand dollars a year, who shares the same conditions, the same hundred dollars can be considered petty change. In the case of these different people, the hundred dollar bill never changes its actual worth, but its perceived value changes with the level of attachment of each individual's consciousness. The survivalist attitude of our social structure skews our understanding of money and turns it into a need that can never be satisfied.

As you advance in your life, you add to the collection of your experiences that continually mold your perceptions and beliefs. With each life situation, you experience lessons. Each lesson adds to the growth of your consciousness through your comprehension of the purpose of the experience; your understanding of the experience allows for further development of your consciousness. As you ascend the ladder of consciousness, you begin to see that individuals resonating at lower levels of consciousness are often a product of their conditioned environment. Separation exists between groups or individuals at this level of perceived survival. At this level, personal judgments and attachments are what dictate the perceived outcome of an individual's thoughts and actions.

We are all capable of any and all actions, whether perceived as good or bad behavior. Your level of conscious understanding dictates your choice of thoughts and actions, which influence your outcomes and experiences in life. Your conscious level of understanding dictates the perception of your actions through your current outlook and the approval of others. Have you ever tried to make up something about yourself in order to grab the attention of another man or woman? Have you ever lied to your partner, friend, co-worker, or employer in order to hide a secret that might make you feel ashamed or feel lesser in the eyes of other individuals? Have you ever boasted or bragged about the amount of money you make, the clothing labels you wear, or name drop the people you know in order to make yourself look and feel more important? When you feed into the illusion of needing to be superior to others, then you are giving away your own energies and letting their approval affect and control you. Seeking or needing the approval of another can hinder your actions and energies because you fall prisoner to the control of their judgment. You imprison the growth of your consciousness. This is commonly seen throughout society, especially within the celebrity culture. When you put people up on pedestals, thinking that they have something special that makes them better than you, you give them your power. You give away the power of yourself. The fear within you, the fear for survival, also fuels the need for approval. When you can separate yourself from the judgment of others, you are able to stand firm in the presence of who you are. Your purpose in life becomes clear.

When you understand that you are the master of your conscious experience and that you can extend past the boundaries of your mental mind, then you can see that only *you* hold yourself back from advancing. You realize that you are only as powerful as you allow yourself to be. When you understand that your limitations are created by your mental boundaries, you realize that you are the creator of your life. How you affect your life and the lives of others is limited by your mental boundaries. We see this in the thoughts and actions of what "I can" and "I can't" do. These simple words remind us of the self-created mental limitations that we place upon ourselves. As you break past these limitations, you become more powerful in your life and in the energy that you put forth. To understand your spirit's potential is to understand who you are and what you can achieve. It is only your mental boundaries that chain you to the belief that you are only human and that you fall under the human laws of human consciousness.

As a child, you understood yourself to be boundless untapped potential. As you grew older, you stepped into society's conditioned paradigms of limitations that caused you to set up your boundaries and fences. To understand that even the fence is an illusion that you have created and accepted for yourself is to understand that the illusion can be dissolved. The boundary exists only within your mind. You can tear down these fences whenever you choose to do so; they were never real to begin with. Hence your thoughts are temporary illusions. This allows you to revert back to your inner childlike state of consciousness, allowing you to experience life without the limitations of judgments that restrict your growth and development. This is once again going back to your original desire or need to experience the reality of your untapped potential. If you use this premise in combination with your animalistic ego nature, then you can direct your energies in whatever direction you want. When combining your ego with the wisdom of your higher intelligence, the two forces have an amazing power. They become your wisdom.

Understand that the role of survival is to drive spirit to exist. It strives for the unionization and integration of the various aspects of who you are. A mother, father, lover, friend, worker, creator, these are various aspects of who you potentially are. Just as great empires are built within the union of the knowledge from separate nations, so the unionization of your chakras can create the full expression and potential of who you are. The animalistic ego is the constant driving force that, when fully evolved through the unification of your spiritual fragments, becomes the full expression of your spirit's wisdom. Existence begins with survival, and is fueled with the emotions of your dreams and desires in order for you to evolve and experience yourself. At first, you might not necessarily know what the best choice for your life is, but as you experience your life, it becomes more clear and measurable. You know this just as you know that feeling good is better than feeling bad. You understand this through the power of your emotions. You know your truth when you feel it inside you.

Understanding of the development of the "emotional body," the second chakra, shows you the power that you hold within your emotions. The emotional development of human existence allows you the ability to empower yourself in every direction possible. Would you like to know the vibrational force that exists within you? Do you want to know how you can energetically affect your environment or become affected by it? It starts with learning through the eyes of a child—your inner child.

CHAPTER 5

SACRAL CHAKRA

The second chakra body, also known as the sacral chakra, is located near your abdomen and sexual organs. It represents the energy flow of your spiritual connection to your human existence through the power of your emotions, thoughts, and intentions. It connects and energetically empowers your spiritual communication and vibrational attraction to the magnetic energy field of your environment. Just as water is a medium that has the ability to support as well as take life, you have the ability to express the many facets of your emotions. It is the stream of consciousness in which your spirit communicates with your physical consciousness and your physical surroundings. Through the second chakra flows the spiritual energy of the emotional body as it expresses itself within your physical identity, a pure expression of the inner child. Like a child that identifies and reacts to her surroundings by expressing her emotions, you communicate energetically your wants, needs, and desires through your energy body within the energy field of your surroundings. Your spirit integrates and communicates information energetically through thoughts, feelings, and emotions within the human experience, as you develop in your physical, mental, and spiritual growth.

So much can be felt and expressed within your emotions; they have incredible power. The joy you feel when hugging someone you love and telling them, "I love you." The anger felt when you experience disappointment, mistrust, or rejection. The feelings in your heart when you experience love, death, or loss. When you connect your thoughts and actions to your emotions, you work from your second chakra body. The second chakra body allows you to attach the energy of your emotions, the energy of your spiritual body, to your physical body as you experience it. It processes and integrates the information from your physical senses into energy.

This is where the word "desire" originates. This is where you feel the power of your emotions that motivate and drive you to experience life and all that it has to offer. Like a child that has no fear unless otherwise taught, you have the desire to live and experience life. Imagine all the sensations the body goes through when you eat a piece of chocolate, listen to your favorite song, or have sex. The degree of energetic information you receive from your physical experiences processes through your body and creates the degree of power felt within your emotions. By attaching emotionally to your experiences, you become the "experiencer" of your life and the mental illusions you create through the development of your emotional body. The degree of empowerment you give to your mental attachments (joy, excitement, drama, pain, and suffering) and how you mentally interpret your experience is referred to as your emotional attachment to the experience. You are the mental experiencer of your physical existence. By initially identifying yourself as the experiencer, you begin your spiritual learning through your energetic energy body. Your attachments to your levels of emotional gratification are linked to your thoughts and actions.

Your emotions and feelings help you consciously (experiencing through the middle self) and subconsciously (experiencing through the inner child) identify with the energy field of your experiences. As you grow and develop, your experiences are what you learn to identify with, validating your physical existence with what you perceptually believe to be real. When reading a book, whether fiction or non-fiction, you can mentally visualize and sometimes identify with the characters or information being conveyed in the written material. You begin to see different degrees of emotions form and unfold when relating to the emotional attachments of the human experience.

Take a neutral example of studying and learning mathematics. The sound principles of numbers, addition, subtraction, division, and multiplication are firmly rooted in all areas of mathematics. To most people, mathematics is not an exciting topic or field of study, but when we begin to see how these basic principles are applied and used in our everyday lives, the importance of mathematics becomes more obvious. Simple mathematics relating to money can have a large emotional attachment to how you live and support your emotional identity. The amount of money you have influences and determines the lifestyle you live, the types of clothes you wear, what car you drive, the kind of home you live in, and the experiences you engage in. The conveniences that surround your life—computers, radio, television, video games—these machines are created through principles of mathematics to determine the structure, programs, power sources, and frequencies necessary to create and run them. The structures of life, the cycles in business, economics, population, agriculture, science, our evolutionary process in relation to life and the universes that surround us, can all be explained and theorized with mathematics. Mathematics is known as a universal language, and just like your emotions, it becomes a big underlying integral part that unifies and allows you to have the physical experiences of life. Similarly, your emotions become the integral part of your physical existence that allows you to connect to your physical life.

To understand the growth and development of the emotional body is to understand how the human body receives and processes information about your environment through the vibrational receptors of your five senses. The five senses of sight, sound, taste, smell, and touch are the body's physical frequency receptors that help you to access and process the information of the energy field around you. The physical senses of the body receive information that you mentally process and consciously attach your emotional energy to, thus you attach energetically to the experience.

We all have a mental baseline over which we perceive as informational overload. When something is too hot, too loud, too bright, too smelly, too sour, or too sweet, the body responds and reacts with an emotional burst of energy. We react by retreating within the protection of our senses: pulling our hand away from the hot handle of a pot, covering our ears, closing our eyes, holding our nose, or spitting our food out. But when we are attuned to these frequencies and become accustomed to them, they become enjoyable, normal, or tolerant to our ability to receive and sense frequencies, just as we can become more accustomed to drinking coffee or wine. Therefore, the emotions and sensations generated within the physical body are freely available for anyone to experience. You process the sensory information of the environment around you in relation to *you*. You choose your mental attachments, or your emotional response to your experience based on your level of exposure, history, or stimulation to your experiences. You choose a degree of happiness, contentment, or sadness anytime you feel the need or desire to express your emotions. You choose how you energetically empower the perception of your experience. It is a subconscious or conscious choice depending upon your own level of awareness. Within higher consciousness, you become increasingly aware of your choices for positive or negative emotions, regardless of the kind of experience you face in life.

Whether you attach to the many different levels of emotional pleasure or pain, the emotional reward, although felt or perceived differently, is in essence the same: an energetic expression within many degrees of love. When you experience acts of violence or injustice, how do you remain conscious, and not attach to or react towards these emotions with an equal or greater negative force? How do you show love in the face of anger, or in the face of your enemies? Master Jesus said to his followers in Mathew 5:38-40, "You have heard that it was said, 'Eye for eye, and tooth for tooth.' But I tell you, do not resist an evil person. If someone strikes you on the right cheek, turn to him the other also. And if someone wants to sue you and take your tunic, let him have your cloak as well. If someone forces you to go one mile, go with him two miles. Give to the one who asks you, and do not turn away from the one who wants to borrow from you." To empower a negative vibration with an equal or greater negative force only allows negativity to grow within you. This negative reaction sends forth its vibration into the world to generate more hatred rather than love and healing. To forgive and accept in the face of negativity is a true expression within the many degrees of love. This is unconditional love. By understanding and mastering the emotional reaction to any experience, whether it is love, anger, resentment, or patience, you are learning the many ways to give, receive, and accept love within the self.

The resistance that you have against your own experiences or those of others in your life represents the degree of resistance you have to feeling wronged inside. It is a mental illusion when you tell yourself you are not capable of performing such acts, or have an inability to allow for forgiveness, compassion, and acceptance for others who have wronged you. When someone steals, lies, cheats, hits, or yells at you, you may feel a sense of being violated. Yet all of us have committed these violations in some degree towards another person at one time in our lives. Some of us may hold on to excuses to justify our reasons for committing negative actions. We were too young and naïve to know the difference or we may not have understood the circumstances behind our reasons to behave so. Perhaps we say to ourselves that it is not the same circumstance or reasoning, and blame it on our past conditioning or upbringing that causes us to do so. If these are the reasons behind your excuses, you are removing your accountability. You are observing a degree of non-acceptance within you. When you don't accept yourself as capable of any and all acts, you can't accept or have compassion for others. Any level of attachment that you create within your emotional memory bank generates a perceived benefit for the self. The way you accept or reject your experiences affects how the energies of the experiences integrate into your memory and knowledge. You hold on to the energies of your rejections that create internal resistance until you are able to accept or fill the energetic void that anchors you to your past. As Master Jesus states in John 8:8, "If any one of you is without sin, let him be the first to throw a stone at her."

If you are able to go through life's experiences without holding on to the emotional anchors of the experience, then you allow the spirit to grow unhindered. If life experiences were as easy as accepting or deleting your life lessons without mentally processing the emotions felt within the experience, then you could easily live life in the balance and acceptance of all things. You wouldn't need to create emotional attachments to remind you of your experiences. When you create emotional attachments to your experiences, it holds you to repeating lessons until you are able to allow yourself to grow emotionally from the lesson of your experiences, thus finally letting go of your attachments. To experience events at the level of your emotions is to process and relive the same events, until you are ready to let go of the emotional energy around the lesson.

At times, you may get caught up or lost in the power of your emotions. Because the power of emotions is so strong, you may believe that the experience of the emotions outweighs the logic of higher consciousness. The degree to which your emotions are felt is like a mirror for you to look into, but you can get lost in multiple reflections by being a mirror to the emotion, rather than understanding it. Until you have truly forgiven and accepted the wrongful acts you've experienced as a lesson, you will hold onto its negative vibration and create energetic scarring within the spirit. It remains an obstacle for you to deal with each time it presents itself energetically in your life. As long as you choose to hold on to the emotional scars of your past, you do not allow them to heal and become smooth within the vibration of your spirit.

If you look at how you learn and advance in any subject, it happens by taking building blocks and adding to them. When you learn basic math, you are then able to advance to algebra. When you have mastered algebra, you learn geometry, then trigonometry, until you have mastered calculus. After you have mastered calculus, you open yourself up to infinite possibilities of advanced mathematical subjects such as astrophysics, theoretical physics, quantum physics, and so on. When learning math, one usually has no emotional attachment to the experience, but accepts the learning process to one's speed and level of comprehension. Try to look at life as learning and acquiring information through the experience process, or the building blocks for physical and spiritual development within the understanding of life. Emotional attachment to any experience means that you have not yet understood or accepted the lesson, but rather you have anchored yourself in the power of your emotions. The acceleration of growth comes from your willingness to learn and accept the lesson or process.

When you hold on to the emotional energy or memory of an experience, you are in essence holding on to the vibrational energy of the emotions attached to the experience. Whether you perceive it as good or bad creates a false identity within the self, for the spirit is not the emotional body. Perceiving something as good or bad at any level hinders the development of your spiritual growth. A person who identifies himself as his life experiences says to the world, "My experiences validate and define who I am." It is validation that says, "Who I am is still living in my past and not the present moment. Who I am now is not whole without the importance of my experiences." You may feel that these feelings and the emotions that are related to past experiences define the identity of growth and development in life, but in actuality they display the degrees of energetic scarring of pain or pleasure that have not been dealt with or let go. Those who define themselves through their experiences follow a path of continual false empowerment within the self and become victims to the illusion of life. Learning and understanding your experiences allows you to know a deeper aspect of your spirit, to continue to grow within your many lifetimes of experiences. Your experiences are lessons to learn from, but they do not define who you truly are—the unlimited potential of spirit.

To be able to feel with your emotions is such a powerful gift to the human experience. When you are in full control of your emotions in the face of any experience, no matter how small or big, you are then able to resonate the true power of divine spirit, the power of presence. The feelings of immortality, invincibility, happiness, peace, nirvana, euphoria, and pleasure are heightened positive expressions of divinity within your emotions. Chasing emotions and feelings can be so powerful that society has created drugs to mimic variations of heightened senses of pleasure or euphoria. Some people use them as a way to set aside daily activities or duties and run away to a place to feel safe and secure as they experience heightened emotional energy. When you become dependent upon seeking heightened sensations to the point of dependency, you begin to lose control of the conscious self and become fully unconscious at the level of survival. All of your energy and focus is directed towards your emotions with the perceived need to feel pleasure in order to survive, which then outweighs the ability to become conscious and aware. At this level, your animalistic ego remains in control of your life and becomes more dominant. You become addicted to physical, chemical, and emotional forms of survival. You are a puppet, an empty shell for the emotional body to run rampant and abuse the self.

At the consciousness level of the sacral chakra, the developing ego has most of its power and authority because it uses the power of emotions. This is where your judgments and personal beliefs are fueled and reinforced through your conditioned morals and beliefs. To this end, you make the majority of your decisions based on your emotions. You have the idea that if you *feel* something is right, then it must be true, but feeling something to be right is only true to the level of your consciousness awareness. The level of what you know or don't know determines your level of comprehension and understanding.

We experience emotional stimulation everywhere we look, on television, in magazines, radios, and ads. The media tell us what we need, what to buy, who to praise for their talents and achievements, and when to shun a person for their so-called faults. Sometimes our emotional conditioning takes hold of us and brings the worst out of us. On the morning of September 11, 2001, terrorists affiliated with al-Qaeda hijacked four commercial passenger jet airliners. The hijackers proceeded to intentionally crash two airliners into each of the World Trade Center towers in New York City, causing the collapse of both buildings and damage to nearby structures. The third airliner was flown into the Pentagon, the United States Department of Defense in Arlington, Virginia. The fourth airliner which was suspected of heading towards the United States Capitol crashed into a near by field outside of Shanksville, Pennsylvania, after passengers and members of the flight crew tried to reclaim control of the plane. The death toll of 9/11 is estimated to be near 2,800 people. The emotional reaction to the aftermath of 9/11 resulted in increased harassment and hate crimes against Middle Easterner minorities in the United States and their places of worship.

If you stop to think about the power of emotions and how they have the ability to control almost all of your thoughts and actions, then you can understand why you find yourself doing outlandish things. When you live out of your emotions, you follow their energetic experience. You become dependent on something to make you feel good about yourself, and if that something isn't going right for you then it brings you emotionally down. This emotional craving can be seen lurking in any facet of your life.

The source of your emotional attachment can be placed upon a pedestal, which represents your false identity. The need to feel good, positive, and energized is falsely empowering your identity towards someone or something outside of you and giving it power over you. You make yourself believe that your own self worth is identified in your actions versus your true worth. When you focus all of your actions and energies into empowering something outside yourself, you create a false emotional perception of who you are. By living out of your emotions, you give away your power of self control. Anything in life will become of great importance to you if you believe it to be so. When you empower these things with the energetic stimulation of your thoughts and emotions, you empower them to greater importance than yourself. A person is only famous if you believe them to be. An item is only worth as much as you value it. This is created by the conditioning of your emotional attachments to your thoughts within the mental beliefs and illusions that you create.

The Buddhist principle of no thought advocates that you detach from your thoughts, your emotions, and thus, your ego. When you start to internalize and busy the mind with thoughts and emotions, you generate temporary energy pockets to fill or smooth the imbalance of your energy body. A smooth energy body creates silence within the mind. Thoughts are created through energetic stimulation or ripples in the energy body. These ripples are the emotional energies held from the past memories of your experiences. These ripples create awareness of imbalance through the busy mind when you are not in acceptance within the self, which reflects your perceptions and judgments outwardly. Without balance and acceptance within the self, you attach to senseless things and then empower them with emotional thoughts. This in turn enables the mind to head in any direction, in order to feel a sense of self-fulfillment or acknowledgment. The mind attaches to the sensory information of the energy field around you for direction, and it holds a multitude of emotional energetic stimulus. People talking, cars moving, lights flashing, sounds blaring, all these sensory stimulations are processed by your physical senses, which can sometimes hit information overload. Your daily experiences provide a choice of emotional attachments that cause you to interact within your environment. However, rather than denying or rejecting your thoughts and emotions, observe them. Your thoughts become an echo of your emotional sensory imbalance within your mind. Observance of your thoughts and emotions shows you where you are currently expressing yourself within your consciousness.

The need or want to be around attractive people, have luxurious things, is in essence desired attention. You don't need to think much at this level of consciousness, because all of your energies are focused and directed towards the soul purpose of pleasuring yourself through the emotional body. To allow yourself to feel an emotion is more concrete then facing a sense of separation identity or lack within you. We live in a world that exposes us to all the things that we think we need or don't have, and therefore, always providing us with a sense of needing an illusion of happiness that is forever changing in the impermanent world around us. We may always be looking or searching for something or someone to fill the void that we feel inside of us because we are spiritually disconnected inside.

Emotionally charged thoughts can take control of your physical actions. Take the example of recognition for our work. Some of us may only need personal satisfaction to validate ourselves emotionally—non-attachment. Others may feel the need to be verbally acknowledged or rewarded for their services—emotional attachment. To the latter, the act of feeling invalidated for their efforts may cause a negative reaction. Complaining to their peers, putting people down, or becoming spiteful is a need of validation when attention is not directed at them to soothe their emotional insecurities. When it comes to accomplishment, they may feel unfairness to such a degree that they might sacrifice their livelihood and do something rash, such as quitting their job. They might even become vindictive or try to sabotage another person's life. Such actions lower a person's vibration to the levels of survival, righteousness, domination, or control.

Take another example: you choose to ask the person you admire out on a date. The outcome could vary from rejection to acceptance, leading you to fuel the experience with emotions of positive or negative attachment. If the outcome is positive, you may be overwhelmed by acceptance of the person; if the outcome is negative, you may feel rejected by the person you initially pursued. You can either end it or take things further. If you look towards the negative in its worst form, you may become obsessed and harbor resentment for the person. You may feel the need to rectify or conquer the situation. You may even revert back to survival consciousness by lowering yourself to the animalistic ego. This can lead to violent acts, such as physical or sexual abuse which are fueled by the desire for self-preservation and conquering. These are only a couple of examples of how emotions can take control of thoughts and make them powerful. This may command you to lose consciousness and allow your emotional energy to inflict harm on you and others around you.

The only control you actually have is the control of your own thoughts, perceptions, actions, and how you empower them with your emotions. If you live your life at the level of survival consciousness, then you will never be capable of finding fulfillment within the self. Lower consciousness of the self relies on continually fulfilling the needs of your emotions, which is forever transient. You become a rash and impatient doer or thinker through your emotions. Your judgment and perceptions emotionally rule your life. When driven by the power of your emotions, combined with your addictions or urges, you succumb to the idea that you need something based out of your emotional need to be soothed versus your rational thinking. When you consider the chemical and physiological reactions that take place when you experience your emotions, you know there is power in your emotions to make your mind and your body feel that something is perceived as necessary. Your belief in this need becomes your false reality. By associating your carnal urges with the emotion of feeling good, whether false or real, you perceive them to be good for you. Emotions can overpower your perceived reality if you do not understand their true role. When drugs, alcohol, or even sex are attached to your emotional instincts, your consciousness goes to its lowest level and becomes a life based upon survival. When it reaches this stage for a lengthy extent, it then becomes an addiction. At this point, you begin to perceive and rationalize it as necessary to the same extent as food or water.

When your emotions become the root of your life, you perceive the act of feeling good as an internal need to be satisfied or fulfilled by an outward attachment. In other words, you allow something outside of you, whether it is an object, person, or experience to have emotional control and power over you because you believe it makes you feel better. This is the basis of false reality, powered by the emotion of the undeveloped ego, which then becomes the center of your focus and the master of your universe. The dominant focus of your mind becomes whatever you attach to as a necessity, versus what is the true reality of your human consciousness: to allow for physical and spiritual growth through the human existence. This relates to the idea that you are what you think and what you think is the reality of your life. The self becomes a prisoner of its false master, the emotional ego. You become living, breathing emotional ego. When you are dependent upon the need to feel good, then your emotions create a rollercoaster ride toward constant fulfillment.

When you desire something in your life, your level of understanding, accountability, and responsibility behind the desire is very important in order to receive it. If you become emotionally attached to something in your life, say wanting a nice car, the degree of your emotional control and attachment to fulfilling this need can unfold in many different ways. The way of achieving your desired outcome is dependent on your level of consciousness that dictates emotional control. The conventional way is to work harder or smarter within your given means and resources in order to purchase the car you want. The car becomes the motivating factor for increasing your monetary production or worth. By applying concepts such as the law of attraction through visualizing and feeling the emotional response of driving the car within your mind and body, you stimulate the power of your mind and body's energy to attract and manifest your desires. This practice is taught by many spiritual teachers and life coaches today. Bestseller books have been written about these concepts and have reached public awareness and mass media.

But what if your emotional desire outweighs your ability to control yourself to be moral? The act of receiving a car can manifest in several ways: purchasing, borrowing, or even stealing the car that you want gives you the same result. The level of your consciousness resonation holds a force of attraction. Your level of consciousness resonation also holds a degree of emotional control in your conscious choice making. In lower levels of consciousness, your ability to control the power of your emotions, your wants and desires, is an attaching force. At higher levels of consciousness, your attraction force is at the level of manifestation. Applying the law of attraction by using the power of your mind and feeling the emotions of receiving in your physical body does work. However, at lower levels of consciousness, it may only bring you more challenging lessons or you may not have the ability to control your emotions enough to be an attracting force. Applying visualization and feeling as a means to evoke the law of attraction is only a small aspect to effectively utilize, draw, and manifest the things that you think or believe you want in your life. Want and desire are based upon your current level of consciousness, and so is the ability to attract. There is much more to the law of attraction then just thinking, visualizing, and feeling in order for it to produce results that actually create the positive impact you may truly desire.

When you have mastered a certain level of consciousness in yourself, in your spiritual evolvement, it creates the presence of manifesting within the level of your spiritual accountability and responsibility to fulfill your want and desire. Skipping steps within the development of your physical and spiritual consciousness voids the law of attraction on a vibrational level. You must also address your many life times of karmic debt and the spiritual contracts that remain unsettled within this life time; these are embedded within each level of consciousness and must be settled before you are able to manifest and create your true potential. This is why you only see a fraction of individuals practicing these methods who are actually able to evoke the law of attraction into physical manifestation. The law of attraction also follows the laws of accountability and responsibility. Taking on power and responsibility at the level of higher consciousness allows the power of your emotions, your spiritual energy, to attract and manifest who you are and everything that you are deserving of. If you attach to your false desires, a negative expression of who you are, it causes negative actions.

Achieving something that you desire makes you feel good about yourself. Each positive experience builds the momentum of positive energy that also creates a level of attraction. When you feel good, you are happy and exude positive energy. People like feeling the energy of positive people. But what happens if you experience negativity in your life? Does your persona change? How do you react? Do you react positively to negative experiences, or do you counteract it with more negativity? Are your emotions created by your exposure to positive or negative experiences? Are you able to accept any experience, whether positive or negative, as a learning experience that is beneficial for your own growth?

Without emotional understanding or control, you can empower yourself falsely. Building momentum in either direction can create power and force, but not having emotional control of yourself gives you a false perception of your emotionally fueled identity. You develop a false sense of identity within your mental perception that creates a false reality of who you think you are. Your life becomes controlled by waves of fluctuating emotions. Your spirit cannot be present without balance; therefore, if you look outward towards happiness, you become an empty desert inwardly, without spiritual presence. Complete happiness is found only from within. If you become dependent on someone or something for your happiness, you become the servant versus the master of the self.

The basic premise in developing your emotions with the ego is to develop your ability to self-motivate in the growth of your consciousness. Within the first three levels of consciousness, the ego perspective initially refers to "me" in reference to the self. When you look for what is best for you versus for the good of all, you become selfish and self-seeking. This little voice inside of you tells you that "me" needs this and "me" needs that. Whatever "me" doesn't have, "me" needs and wants. Why? Because the "me" becomes your measure based on emotional needs, whether they are physical, material, emotional, or chemical. When you satisfy your current needs, you then find new ones; this continuously creates small and often meaningless temporary identities. If you perceive yourself through the eyes of everyone else, you exclude yourself and see yourself as insignificant. You then rely on the approval and the measure of others in order to create your own self-worth. Your definition of success fluctuates and depends on what and with whom you attach your self-worth.

What does it really mean to be happy? What does it mean to be complete? What does it mean to survive? If your true basic necessities were simplified, you would realize that you don't need much in order to succeed in life. When you only search for fulfillment outside of yourself in order to find happiness, then you are merely looking for the acceptance of another's approval. You create non-acceptance within yourself.

It is your social paradigm that stimulates the perceived lack within your own consciousness, which is what the majority of the people in the world are exposed to. Regardless of race or cultural differences in the world, we all live, eat, and breathe. When you attach to your environment, you take on the social perceptions based on your conditioned needs within that environment. As you follow your path through life, you are in discovery of who you are. Additionally, you can only raise your level of consciousness based upon your willingness to step out of the boundaries of your social paradigms and think for yourself. You can then ask what "I" can do to improve "me" in order to benefit the "we," which is the will of your higher consciousness.

When you look outside yourself, you are driven by others to motivate your psyche and your senses. If you are continually looking externally for answers to your inner peace, then you are learning about another person's journey. By not answering your questions with your *own* answers, you are not honoring yourself. If you look at the premise within the majority of philosophies and religions, they all teach the same principles, to turn inward and follow your higher will and what is best for you. The first commandment states in Exodus 20:3, "Thou shalt have no other Gods before me." Meaning, do not follow, worship or covet anything outside of you. If you worship other objects, idols, gods, or people, then you are following the story of another person's path towards their self discovery or connection. The truth of your path is that you hold the answers to your own path. Therefore, instead of attaching outwardly for validation, learn to listen to your higher self, the God within you.

By surrendering to yourself, you are empowered to come forth and seek the true answers from within. When you realize that you are pure energy and are connected to and come from a divine vibration, you are able to obtain higher consciousness and raise your vibrations to the level of your highest potential. When you focus your intent to this level of understanding, you tell your spirit that you are ready to learn how to grow. You attract the people and things needed to manifest and follow the path that you have chosen for yourself. You step out of your lower levels of consciousness and are no longer dependent upon your emotions to direct the ego and your motivations. The ego now becomes the driving force that works with your higher, faster vibrating frequency. You develop the self while developing the ego. At lower levels of consciousness, you enable the ego to control you by allowing your emotions to take over and become the measure for your needs, wants and desires. The ego at this level controls your world and all that you seek and desire for yourself. When understood and developed properly, the ego becomes the discernment of your wisdom.

When you give full control to your emotions, you are no longer able to make conscious decisions for your own good. You are controlled by neediness and desires, which are false realities. You do not need anything other than the basics of existence. You can advance in order to serve your higher good, but when you advance out of needs and wants, they become your false perceptions that you create as your reality. Your reality therefore is driven by following false needs to obtain your wants and desires. When you give away your power to your emotions, to people or things you perceive as important, you create false gods. You are no longer in control of your life. You become a follower of false realities, which serves no one except your false ego. This is not to say that it is not good to have or experience material goods or conveniences in life. Allowing yourself to enjoy worldly goods and luxuries is perfectly acceptable within the context of self-enjoyment, rather than for approval or self-validation. And of course, balance is always healthy, because excess begets addiction, and addiction takes control of your life to where you are no longer able to see what is good for you or those around you.

When you ground yourself in your desires and you desire things that may educate or improve your life, you are able to affect your life and the lives of others in a positive manner. When you are in control of your emotions, then your motivations take you in positive, non self-serving, directions. When you choose your life versus your life choosing you, then you take on the responsibility for your world and how you choose to live in it. You add to the vibration of the Earth as a whole, instead of taking away from it and draining others. This gives you a positive vibration that is nurturing and attractive to others. You are able to serve the world. You are able to live as an adult rather than a child who constantly needs attention. The whole purpose of life is to learn and grow from life's experiences, whether physical or spiritual. You can grow and nurture the people around you. In this sense, we become the keepers of the world as well as its teachers. We step out of learning lessons of karma that are continually repeated within our lives. We see the value of the lesson versus the end result. We become students of spiritual advancement versus people who are manipulated by circumstance.

The ego and your emotions are necessary to measure the result of your success. When used appropriately, you can leverage your ego and emotions in a positive direction, as opposed to an uncontrollable rollercoaster ride of confusion. You can choose to feel free and balanced, or caged and unsettled. When you find inner peace, you find yourself. You allow yourself to live in control of your life in a positive sense and no longer give in to petty desires. You are unhindered by perceived setbacks and you build strength in the lessons you've learned, whether negative or positive. You take control of your life and choose to live out of acceptance and abundance rather than living for the end result. You are freed from greed, coveting, and false desires or realities. You live your life for the betterment of the whole. When you increase your level of consciousness, you take control of your life and no longer need to repeat lessons that you may view as continual mistakes.

When you act without thinking and know that you are doing something that isn't in your best interest, you are satisfying the needs of your emotional body. To do something to satisfy your immediate needs is to function out of the animalistic nature that supports your emotional satisfaction. When you consciously recognize this level of resonation, then you can identify with the cause of your neediness to learn and advance to the next level of understanding. When you understand the different levels of consciousness within yourself, you can work within your means. This allows consciousness to work for you rather than against you. By recognizing and letting go of emotional attachments to the consequences of your actions, you can understand how to resonate at all levels simultaneously and function as a whole being rather than as a fragmented individual. To understand the drive of the emotional body is to develop a two-way relationship of parenting.

Your animalistic urges can serve you in any direction that you focus your intentions. The perception of the ego serves your emotional purposes. At what point does striving for what you want become unhealthy or wasteful to you or others in your life? The ego can be a very powerful instrument at any level of consciousness if you understand how to use it and where to direct it. It is the basic premise of your body's survival and existence, a reflection of your level of consciousness. In experiencing the power of your emotions, you begin to develop a reference point for balance and variation within your life experiences. Within the experience there is always a degree of understanding and wisdom, no matter how great or how small that experience is. The measure of your experience holds a degree of separation from previous experiences of your past. When you begin to understand the lesson behind your experiences, you begin to acknowledge who you are, and you begin to form your mental identity or "mental body." As you gain acceptance within the self, you develop the intellect of your mental body, the part of you that balances between the intellect of your emotions and your wisdom to decide what is right for you. Within the development of your identity, you begin to hold the strength and power of who you are, both mentally and emotionally. The mental development of who you are is the next step in evolving your physical and spiritual growth.

CHAPTER 6

SOLAR PLEXUS

The third chakra body, also known as the solar plexus, is located at your navel. As fire has the ability to forge various physical elements into form, structure and physical identity, the solar plexus forges the thoughts and emotions of your experiences into creating your physical identity through the "mental body." Within the development of your mental body, you begin to conceptualize, define and further direct your self identity to assist your physical life and your purpose. This is driven by the strength of your developing ego as it directs your mental body to mold and define your identity, function, power, control, and freedom to be you, to engage the power of one.

Ask yourself, "What do I think about how I live my life? What motivates me to move forward in life?" However you answer these questions, you are most likely using part intuition, part intellect, but mostly an ego approach that is based upon your emotional drive to propel yourself forward. This approach can be healthy or harmful depending upon how you are motivated. The decision starts with the development of your intellect within the mental body, where you are in your life, and what it is that you perceive as important. The things that you feel you need for your own survival dictate the desires of your actions. It is your ego nature that drives you to believe that you are doing these things for your own good and possibly for the good of others. In most cases, your motivations dictate the decisions that you choose on a day-to-day basis. Your desires give you a general direction about where you are heading in life and the experiences you choose to take on.

When you realize where you are at in your level of consciousness, you can consciously decide what it is that you are trying to achieve. This is the main objective of the human intellect and your daily decision process. Even if you base your decisions on principles or moral beliefs, they can still be emotionally conditioned to your attachments. You are processing through the understanding within your own level of intelligence. When you understand the power of your emotions and how you utilize them in your everyday life, you can direct the ego instead of the ego directing you. When you rise above the levels of survival and emotion, you begin to feel a sense of identity and control within the self. You begin to empower your mind as well as body. You begin to make positive decisions for yourself that help to enhance your intellect, your function, as well as your physical life and well-being. You come to the realization that there are infinite possibilities before you in which you may choose to take control of your life or become a by-product of your environment. You begin to mentally exercise the mind as well as take care of the temple that houses the spirit, and become the keeper of your physical body. Choice is the first step toward making the right decisions for your life in advancing spiritually, intellectually and physically. It allows you to move toward self-improvement and the doorway which recognizes that "God, Spirit or Source" is near, whether you consider that within or outside of you.

When you engage with the intellect rather than your emotions, you realize that you are more than the desires of your emotions. You empower yourself using the human will that is supported by your conscious and subconscious intellects. It is the will and intellect of an individual that separates one person from another and forms a person's unique identity. The formation of your identity creates separation between you and others, urging you to develop and grow your own special characteristics and gifts to offer to the world. This allows you to utilize, form and create the things to better yourself and improve your daily life. If you choose to believe in something and empower it, then you can take the necessary steps to achieve it. This is the intellect of the human mind, a mind of "works."

In this way of thinking, you come to believe in the ability of "works." You believe that the things you do to improve yourself will better your life and the lives of the people that surround you. You begin to act within the community by developing long-term goals to improve your life and your livelihood. You realize that if you enhance your intellect and grow both mentally and physically, you can achieve a better community for you or your family, whether it is your nucleus or your supportive environment. You look to and depend on others as well as a sense of inner or outer forces to help guide you. You step into the adolescent phase of spiritual growth, learning by trial and error and feeling assisted by a more powerful source—the recognition of the "Spirit" or "God." These are all stages in developing physical consciousness with spiritual consciousness within the third chakra and the mental body.

It starts with treating the mind and body as a sacred temple. By eating correctly and taking the appropriate nutrition that your body requires, you improve its form, function, and performance. When you take care of yourself, you feel better; the way you look and feel projects outwardly in your behavior and confidence. By taking care of yourself both mentally and physically, you have respect for who you are and what you have to offer to the world. You can then begin working on your intellect through experiencing different lessons and situations encountered in life. Depending upon the attachment to your experiences, you may choose to direct your mind and enter different areas of study. The more you learn, the more you fine tune your intellect to incorporate into your life path. As you further develop your intellect, you begin to resonate and attract your current life's purpose and path. You begin to specialize in different fields that build the foundation of your life and your livelihood. You gain access to your unique gifts and manifest skills that are engrained within you. You come into this life complete with all of your gifts and abilities acquired and obtained throughout your many lifetimes; it is only a matter of allowing, acknowledgement and practice to access and express your abilities. You contribute to the world and enhance yourself and the people around you. The formation of the mental body of the human intellect is what separates you from your animalistic nature as well as your undirected desires. It allows you to begin to formulate the identity of who you are and what it means to be you.

As humans, we live our lives through our experiences and how we were raised socially and culturally. Life begins based upon these acquired foundations, but there are other spiritual factors that play a role in determining how your life and physical identity unfold. From the moment you are born—time, day, month, and even year—you leave yourself clues to who you are or were spiritually, prior to coming into your physical body. As you enter your physical life, you choose the parents that could teach you the traits that are similar to your present spiritual nature so that you can continue your work on the journey of improving your knowledge and experiences carried forth from your spiritual essence. This also allows you to learn the lessons that your spirit deemed necessary to overcome or achieve within your current life. If parents think back to when their children were still in the womb, they can see that energetically the children hold similar characteristic traits and mental issues that they, as parents, were dealing with at the time of conception and pregnancy.

From the womb, infants can sense through their mother by sensing the energy of her vibration. From conception, infants are comforted with knowing that she has taken care of them while they were still developing into human form by providing nourishment, warmth, safety and protection. They also experience intellectual and emotional growth from her everyday activities, through the vibration of her interactions. Many modern books and studies advise us that we can communicate with our children before they are born. Our own spiritual and emotional vibrations, physical ingestion and intellectual stimulation are all being taught to our children while still in the womb. The child in the womb enters into the body at the parents' levels of consciousness vibration and takes on the resonation of their conscious state at that period of time. This in effect causes the child to take on the parents' emotional characteristics, stability and personal issues that are akin to them, as well as those that remain unresolved. Just like an infant who is born of a mother with an alcohol or chemical dependency, so does a child have a greater chance of developing the same human addiction through the direct ingestion or exposure of the toxins in the blood stream that is exchanged between mother and child.

As parents encounter their feelings and experiences of joy or suffering, they take on the vibration of the experience and expose the same vibrational experience to the unborn child through their chosen actions, thoughts, emotions and experiences. This is why, when we have more than one child at different points in our lives, we can see that they hold and take on different characteristic traits and personas that are a cumulative reflection of the experiences that we exposed ourselves to during that particular time of pregnancy. This energetic informational exchange begins the development of our physical and behavioral identity as the spirit enters the physical existence. We often hear parents make remarks such as, "He has your temper," or "She has my artistic ability." Every level of consciousness that is developed and obtained leads us one step closer to our true identity. Learning to master your physical realm is a process of responsibility.

At this third level of consciousness development, you are aware that you are the human creator of your physical realm. You take on the physical attributes of what you do and accomplish in life. What you receive is based on your own merits. You think this way because you direct and empower your ego in wanting to improve yourself intellectually. You empower thoughts and judgments within the direction that empowers your intent and focus of your energies. You may perceive your accomplishments and your education as what separates you from the person standing next to you. You stand within your own self-created pride based on your level of achievements. You believe you are only as important as you and others view you, although this is a false perception of your true identity.

The gathered lower consciousness of the solar plexus is the root of your physical identity and how you perceive yourself in the eyes of others. How you empower yourself consciously and emotionally dictates how you affect everyone you encounter either positively or negatively. Imbalanced energies within your third chakra can also affect the desired outcome of your decision-making, causing lower levels of attraction, like attracting like-minded, and creating undesired or forced outcomes. However, if you are able to center yourself, then you are able to harness your own powers and draw to you the things you want or desire in life. This, in effect, nullifies your perceived needs and sends you further along your path toward the identity of who you truly are.

If you stand within your own power, then you attract the things that are already yours. You cannot be anything that you already are not. Through your life experiences you eventually evolve into the only person that you are capable of being: you. In this way, you can repel the things that don't belong to you, reducing the lessons you need to learn in life. When you are happy and content, your energy increases and becomes free and overflowing, thereby attracting abundance into your life, you feel complete. When you are experiencing a sense of need or want in your life, whether it is mental, emotional, physical or material, you are in essence feeling a sense of lowered or uneven energy within your own spirit's capacity. This causes you to seek outwardly to temporarily fulfill the void within in order to feel complete or worthy—in essence, full.

To understand your true identity is first to understand where you came from. We have a tendency to believe that we, as humans, have a right to separate ourselves from each other based on our achievements and activities. This separation, nevertheless, only defines what validates us externally. What we have and the things that we do can change in an instant if we lose the capability to mentally or physically perform our individual responsibilities. While some define themselves by titles and achievements, others tend to define who they are based on color, culture, heritage, and ancestry. Hypothetically, life began with the procreation of two people, flourishing into the billions of people that exist on the planet today. So the question remains, who are we?

Identity is first and foremost a false reality. Whenever you need to identify or label something or someone, you place your own judgments and perceptions into your evaluations, which are falsely self-created. When you do this, you base your perceptions on your attachments to your belief systems, which constantly evolve and change. What you believed to be true as a child was based on the consciousness level of your parents' social perceptions and conditioning. What you believe to be true today is based upon your experiences and the level of your *own* consciousness. With the accumulation of new experiences, relationships, and studies, you continually mold and develop your understanding of what is true and what is possible. Truths and realities constantly change through the growth and development of the mental body. Therefore, identity is a false reality because it is always based on impermanence and perspectives, on ideas and judgments that are bound to time and changing points of view.

Remember that you are, in essence, a vibrational spiritual being. You are part of and connected to everything vibrationally; therefore, you have no separation and no identity. If you can imagine and understand this, then you will see that you are continuous flowing energy both in your physical and spiritual being. Taken a step further, thoughts and judgments can add to or take away from your own energy vibrationally. The more emotional charges that you add, the greater the charge becomes and, therefore, begins to attract the outcome that you've generated for yourself. If you can conceive of this idea, you can see how you are responsible for all of your actions. You should take on your responsibilities rather than removing acceptance and adding blame when something doesn't perceptually turn out the way you desire.

As you raise your vibrations through the directed intentions of your thoughts and actions, you begin to attract and resonate with people of similar vibrations. You choose who you want to teach and learn from in your life and what lessons you feel like taking on or experiencing. You decide how you perceive, attach and interact with your surroundings. Everything else is out of your control. The irony is that we exist in an environment that allows us to become perceived doers or watchers of our own life paths. Because we are in false perceived control of our own lives, we live life ignorantly based on our own glorification and believe there is a higher power that watches over us. The act of your personal free will is merely the freedom to choose how you want to perceive, react or attach to something that simply exists. The world around you is forever changing; you simply self-create the experience that you want to allow yourself to receive. This reception depends on how you attach to the experience. As you evolve your levels of consciousness further, you eventually become your true identity: the triune of your own divine self.

You live in a world that teaches you that you need to feel good and look better than everyone else by acquiring more and more things to define your own identity. If stripped of all of your material wealth, you are only separated by your intellect to recreate yourself. If stripped of your intellect then all you have is an empty shell of living flesh that seeks for survival. What remains is the original vibration of consciousness within the spirit. Spirit then chooses whether to project itself into the flesh to learn and experience through the knowledge of the energy field within the physical existence. In the true reality within the consciousness of the experience, you discover that you are complete within yourself once you are able to recognize the self. When you no longer need to attach to the illusion of the mental mind and your environment for validating your own self worth, you then become truly conscious. When you move past the attachments of your judgments, perceptions and emotions, you live life by being present and allow your life to unfold and manifest the recognized force and intelligence that is within all of us. This leads you closer to knowing what is most important—connection, compassion, and love: the matters of the heart.

CHAPTER 7

HEART CHAKRA

The fourth chakra body, also known as the heart chakra, is located in the heart/chest region. The heart chakra is the central chakra of the seven chakra system in the lower self. It is the bridge that connects your physical self to your spiritual self. It unites the mind, body and spirit, masculine and feminine, persona and shadow. It begins to create unity with your ego as you learn self-acceptance and gain confidence in who you are. As air has the means to circulate itself and affect the environment around us, when you achieve the level of heart consciousness, you begin to integrate who you are within your environment. Your energies begin to integrate and support the overall consciousness of your environment and the people within it. You begin to empower not only yourself, but the people around you. You provide the support, strength, and connection that build your higher emotions to give way to love and compassion in the development of you and your community—the power of many.

The heart chakra is one of the most powerful chakra bodies of the lower self. The lower self is the physical expression and existence of your spirit that allows your spirit to learn and grow from your physical experience. The heart chakra is the part of the spiritual body that balances and connects your masculine and feminine energies, as well as connects your physical body to the power of your spiritual energy body. When you feel your emotions as you experience life, you feel the many different degrees of joy or pain. You feel the energy of your spiritual body resonating the energy of your emotions within your heart. These emotional energies are the energy shifts of your energy body as it connects itself energetically to your physical body through your heart chakra. The joy that you feel when you are happy or excited after you achieve a goal, reward, or accomplishment is created by the energy spikes of your spiritual body. The closeness that is felt when you share intimacy or connection with someone you love is the communion and integration of two energy bodies sharing each others' energy fields. The pain that is felt when you feel sad or disappointed is the lull of energy within your spiritual body.

Just as your blood is circulated through your body by your heart, the energy of the spiritual body is circulated by your heart chakra through the major chakras, meridians and minor chakras of your spiritual body. The energy shifts that occur in your energy body are felt through your physical body by the energies that create your emotions. All the feelings within your heart are made up of the energy moving through your energy body. Fueled by the power of your emotions, your mind and body receives information as you attach and connect to your life experiences. When you are finally able to control the power of your emotions rather than your emotions controlling you, you begin to develop your higher emotional energies of love, compassion, abundance and acceptance, moving beyond desire, selfishness, greed and control.

When thinking about where emotions are felt and displayed, we like to reference that our feelings come from the heart, even though we know scientifically that the majority of emotional physiology is produced by chemical reactions found within the brain. So why do we always reference the heart as the place where we hold our feelings? Emotions are, in essence, the energy you create that integrates the energetic sensory information of your experiences. The heart chakra is the energetic center that bridges your physical body to your spiritual body (your energy body). Your energy body relays the information of the magnetic energy field around you and processes this information to your physical body through your heart chakra. This then creates the energies of your emotions that circulate through your etheric body via your heart chakra. The emotional energy felt within your heart resonates and circulates the informational sensory energy of your experience through the emotions felt within your body. The specific emotions that you create and feel are based on your level of consciousness. The heart chakra is where you energetically bridge your mental connections to your physical connections when experiencing and interacting with people and relationships. Feelings of love, trust, and honor support the strong energetic bonds that build strong connections between people in healthy relationships.

Your heart chakra is the bridge that connects the spiritual self to the physical self; it allows your physical body to coexist with your spiritual body. It integrates your masculine and feminine energies in harmony, in order for you to express and nurture yourself within your surroundings. The heart chakra acts as the channel that merges your spiritual world and your physical world within your path of consciousness development.

The lower half of your first seven chakra bodies, chakras one through four, represents the growth and development of your spirit in the preparation of your human existence. The information within your first four chakras prepares your spirit to exist in the physical world and allows you to adapt and survive within your physical environment. The upper half of your seven chakra bodies, chakras four through seven, prepares your human existence to reintegrate itself to your spiritual existence. It does this by engaging your intuitive nature to access the information and abilities held within multiple past life experiences immersed within your energy body. As you raise your level of consciousness, you raise your spiritual awareness that unfolds hidden gifts and talents waiting to be discovered inside you.

Everyone has a set of talents or skills that they are good at. These are the things that come easy and natural to them, while others may have a more difficult time in learning or grasping the same ability or concept. Even though the majority of us have the same physical attributes, we are all built a little differently in our intellectual and physical makeup; that makes us special and unique individuals. Some people have the gift of song in their voice, while others have the ability to teach or communicate effectively to individuals or large groups. Some people can easily understand and assimilate mathematics, while others can disassemble and reassemble automobile engines with little help or guidance.

These gifts are your innate attributes that unfold within the development of your intellectual and spiritual growth. Your gifts and abilities help you direct your life purpose and give you glimpses of who you are and what you are here to do. These innate abilities within you are the abilities that you have to offer and share within your community. They also allow you to connect to others in order to further learn and unfold who you are. The relationships that you create help you build higher emotions that enhance your spiritual growth and development. Creating connections and relationships to other people expands your knowledge of who you are. It allows you to experience more of yourself and creates a deeper connection with your heart.

So what does it mean to be connected with your heart? This statement is simplistic, but as you may know, the action is more complicated. In order to achieve anything in life, you must be grounded and centered within yourself. Everything in your life starts and ends with you. From the moment you wake up, every decision you make affects the direction of your life's path. To understand this is to understand the power of your perceived "free will" and how it resonates with your level of consciousness. The survival consciousness within you believes that you control your life through your mere acts of choice, influenced by thoughts, emotions and actions that you perceive and act upon. When you work out of your lower levels of consciousness, you become more self-serving to your personal needs and desires. You believe that you are the driving force and creator of your physical reality. You create your life through the information you receive from physical senses which create and develop your human intellect. Your senses process the information of you in your environment. When you are able let go of your need to control, your mental perception changes to awareness. You begin to realize that you are more than your physical presence. You come to realize that every thought, word and action exchanges fundamental energies that contributes or takes away energy from you and your environment. As you develop your higher emotions, you unfold higher levels of consciousness within you. You begin to realize that there is a greater presence that orchestrates and supports the world around you.

To recognize that there is something far greater than your physical self is the first step in opening the doorway to higher consciousness. Whether you want to call this God, Buddha, chi, universal consciousness, or a greater force, you begin to see that you are not in complete control of your life or your surroundings. Life and everything that exists all around you continues its existence whether or not you choose to participate and be present within it. The cars driving down the streets, the people talking in restaurants and coffee shops, the birds flying through the air, they exist and continue to exist independent of you. They do not need your permission, approval, or presence for their existence. They only have your attention or awareness of their existence when you choose to acknowledge their presence. You are only in control of your chosen mental attachments, the thoughts and actions that you create in order to view the picture or illusion that you create in your mental mind.

The need to think that you are in control of your life creates resistance within the energies that support you. These are the same mental energies that confine you and hold you back with the fear of needing to be in control. It is the same resistance that is felt when someone is trying to manipulate or control you through force. Whether it is physical, mental, or verbal abuse, it leads you to harbor lower emotions that create anger, shame, resentment, insecurity, uncertainty, and doubt within yourself. These are the same lower emotional energies that destroy friendships, partnerships, and communities—the power of being one. Allowing for things to exist within their own presence and expression is the ability to let go of your need to control who you are. In recognizing your need to control, you begin to recognize the resistance that you have within yourself that you may also be projecting onto those around you. This frees you from the lower emotional energies that bind you to survival. Acceptance gives you permission to expand and grow.

In releasing your need to control, you accept responsibility for your choices. In recognition and acceptance of your resistance, you can choose not to remain a victim or prisoner to your mental boundaries. When you let go of resistance, you free up the emotional energy that you use to force you to act and react to your surroundings. Have you ever been driving along and all of the sudden a rock flies out of nowhere and chips your windshield? It always comes as a shock when you hear the sound of a loud noise or something flying into your field of vision, causing you to swerve, brake, or pause for a moment. The reaction that takes place after the incident can unfold in many directions, depending on your conscious level of awareness. Some people get angry and begin to curse the rock, some people get upset at themselves wondering why these things always happen to them, and some continue on their way knowing that they need to simply get the windshield fixed for their own vision and safety. Your reaction to events in your life reveals the degree of energetic imbalance that you have in your spiritual body. This creates the expression of your emotions that causes you to put your mind and thoughts on hold as your mental focus attaches to your experiences. The degree of your emotional hiccup shows a hidden lesson of resistance and control within yourself.

As you free the energies that bind you to emotional anchors of your past, no matter how big or small, you allow yourself to be open to learning and growing. Being free of stale emotional energy allows you to add new energy and new growth into your life. Within existence is the presence of being that allows you to integrate with the energies around you in order to feel life. It is your conscious level of understanding and involvement that dictates the mental picture that you add to your physical experience. Once you begin to let go of your need to control, you step into learning from your spirit. Surrendering your need to control allows for you to die to the self (your physical self) and be born into spiritual self-awareness. You recognize that there is something more than you, more than your physical life. You then acknowledge and integrate your spiritual energy with the magnetic energy field that surrounds you, that greater force that you came from. Connecting to this greater presence allows you to evolve into something greater than what you already are. You become higher consciousness.

The physical experience allows you to learn and understand the development of your consciousness. You are in control of your thoughts and emotions. You choose your mental attachments and empower them with your emotional energies. Your physical life is a reflection of the energies of your developing consciousness—the thoughts, emotions and beliefs that are engrained within you. When you realize that these things do not define who you are, you gain acceptance and have awareness within you. You realize that everything has a growth and learning process for its own expression. When you no longer feel the need to edit your internal world, your mental thoughts and emotions, you stop trying to figure out the movie and enjoy your life. Slicing up the film of your perception in order to create the perfect image or movie for you to replay in your mental mind creates stale energy or roadblocks in your life. The mind is merely a projection of your internal thoughts that you play for your personal need or enjoyment.

When you then begin to recognize the difference between positive and negative energy, forces of flow, you label and define them out of judgment from experience. When you recognize and identify with positive or negative energies, you project them in your thoughts, beliefs and perceptions. You then create identification, reasoning and labels that form your belief systems and define your reasoning. Since most of us do not understand the positive and negative energy flows of the spirit, we define things within our personal set of morals and judgments. Have you ever met someone for the first time and immediately disliked him for no apparent reason? Even though you do not have any past history or experience with this person, you feel a sense of uneasiness around them or within their presence. When you meet people that you do get along with, you feel the connection of similar resonations that allows you to learn from each other and the things you both have to offer one another. This becomes a learning exposure to energy flows, your discernment to the human vibration and energy flow that people release from their energy body.

As a child, you were controlled by the emotions of your experiences. Why are there children who are fearless when riding off jumps on their roller blades, skateboards, bikes and snowboards, while others are terrified of such feats? The thrill, excitement or fear of the experience is based upon the level of personal enjoyment that you attach to the experience. Your determination is based upon your level of desire and emotions tied to what you want to experience. What excites you, troubles you, or stops you is your emotional attachment. Within the learning process of the experience, you often may stumble or fall, leading to cuts, bruises, scars and sometimes broken bones that remind you of the learning process within the experience.

This is the same path that your emotional evolvement takes as it grows and develops within your life experience, from your second chakra to your fourth. Within the development of the second chakra, you are controlled by your emotions. Within the heart chakra, you learn to control your emotions so they lead you to the higher emotions of love and connection, connecting your awareness to your higher spiritual fragments. It is this same ability to get up from a fall when you feel pain, to not give up, to continue to experience life that drives you forward. This is the spiritual force within you, and comes with the innate knowledge that you have the ability to empower yourself until you are able to master yourself.

When you begin to empower yourself from the heart, you start with the recognition of your self-worth. To know who you are is to know and accept yourself. Seeing yourself as an important and worthy individual, equal to all others, allows you to contribute to the environment around you. You empower yourself with your thoughts and actions, giving you the ability to see and feel for yourself. With the recognition of who you are, you are able to affect the world around you. How you choose to empower your life affects the energies around you. With self-empowerment, you are able to believe in and utilize your strengths and grow the energies of your power and presence. Accepting the idea that you are more than your physical life allows you to connect to a greater presence, which enables you to access the higher levels within your consciousness. When you create mental boundaries of physical and spiritual separation, you limit your spiritual growth. Separation becomes the anchor of most philosophies and religions that believe and worship a higher power. However, your internal truth defines your beliefs and limitations. Your self-created truths can limit or hold you back from understanding the reality of who you are, who you believe yourself to be within your own physical, conditioned mind.

The first step in finding your true self begins with your own self-perception and the relationship you have with yourself. How you view yourself and those around you is a mirror image of how you perceive yourself. The things you dislike about others are a reflection of what you have internally separated or have not accepted as possible within you. If you are vibrationally connected to everything, then you are a part of everything and everything is a part of you. Your perception and judgment mirrors your level of consciousness awareness. Within the ability to experience a full spectrum of existence, accepting everything from light to dark, you expand your understanding. When you can learn to love yourself unconditionally, then you can love and accept everything around you unconditionally and remain a balanced force of energy that contributes to the balance of the universe and the energies around you. The things you identify and resonate with most give you an image of how you currently view your inner core beliefs that reflect outwardly into your physical life. Your emotions do not dictate your consciousness, but enforce your level of understanding within you. Your level of consciousness is seen within your mental attachments to people, things or experiences that favor certain morals or beliefs. In order to overcome these obstacles within yourself, you learn through exposure and gain deeper understanding and compassion through life's experiences that continually remold your perception of truth.

As an example of how perceptions evolve with greater understanding, when society was first exposed to the knowledge of AIDS in the 1980s, tremendous fear was created around this unknown virus that was causing an increasing amount of death within the gay population of our communities. Eventually, the disease spread and inserted itself into the general population through the spread of sexual contact, needles and blood transfusions. Society's initial attachments to the fear of the unknown created a lot of anger, prejudices, judgment and blame. Within the last few decades, although we still have not created a cure for this disease, society has learned and educated itself through continual exposure and experience within the fears of AIDS in order to come to a better understanding and comfort level with this disease.

Through self-acceptance, you begin to move toward your true identity. You grow in unison with both the mental intellect and the wisdom that resides in your spirituality. You begin to learn from a part of you that is connected to something greater, older and wiser. You begin to connect to your higher source. Whether you want to call this God, Buddha, or spirit, it is your higher self. The more you experience yourself, the more love and affinity you have for the teachings of your higher source. It begins to trigger a connection within you. It creates a connection with your spirit that guides your life.

To be able to take on more power within you requires more responsibility and accountability. When you become a parent for the first time, you take on the responsibility of a human life and its development. When you start your own business, you take on the responsibility of the direction and growth of the company. The greater the responsibilities you take on for yourself, the less room you have for removing the comforts of irresponsibility or blame. You have only to look at yourself and who you choose to support your choices and experiences. In the end you have only yourself to be responsible for taking on the responsibility of your true power—your spirit.

Moving beyond these limitations, the next step towards identifying yourself as whole brings you to the journey within to discover the truth of who you are. They say the longest road traveled is the shortest path taken as you reconnect the separation of your mind and heart. If the mind remains conditionally bound, then the heart is ruled by its boundaries and its mentally reinforced conditions. It is the perception of the mind that dictates the feeling of the heart. Your mind can only comprehend what it logically understands, what it is conditioned to believe is moral or immoral, right or wrong, good or bad. Being exposed to experiences, whether they are easy or difficult, gives you the choice of learning and overcoming them or remaining stuck within your emotional attachments. When you are able to remold your mental perception, you are then able to identify with another person that may be suffering from the same experiences. There becomes less and less separation between you and other people's experiences

Emotional attachments are empowered by your thoughts with the power of energy from your emotions. When your thoughts are positive, you increase the vibrations of your own energetic fields. Similar to the effects of exercise, increased positive vibrations have been shown to raise our immunities, bodily functions, as well as our energy levels. When you harbor negative thoughts with emotions, then you may empower yourself within negative energy fields that cause unwarranted stress, fatigue, depression, and possible illness or disease within the body. In other words, the energies that you empower the body with, both physically and mentally, can affect the overall form and function that pertains to its health. Through the experience of your attachments, the body becomes the vehicle that houses these energies. Simply stated, the perception of your thoughts and judgments dictates how you interact in your social and physical environments.

Within your mental perception, your physical life is sometimes falsely identified as the foundation of who you are. However, the perception of your life does not necessarily correlate to who you are spiritually. Not all paths toward finding oneself or achieving enlightenment are the same. Enlightenment phonetically states, "In the light you were meant." Within this spiritual light, you find your true self. As you travel down the path toward reconnecting back to your true self, you begin to see all that is good and feel all that is wondrous. As you raise your own vibrations, you connect more to the light from which you came and from which you were meant to return.

This resurrection of the spirit from within, at the consciousness development level of the heart chakra, allows you to reconnect back to your source of creation—your spirit. In the light you were meant to be, and when you leave your physical body, in the light you will return.

What you experience in this life is recorded within the genetic makeup of your spirit, which adds to or removes from your spiritual karma. The energies that you send forth through your positive or negative actions and intentions generate the energies that make up your karma and the development and attraction of your energy field. Therefore, as your spirit experiences and grows in the physical existence, you add to your spiritual development. Not all of us are meant to be saints and not all of us are meant to be sinners. These are merely labels to which society has placed judgments and conditions on the controlled mind. You act selflessly or selfishly depending upon your own level of awareness and where you begin your spiritual journey.

Remember that there is no right or wrong to the way you live your life, there are merely positive or negative choices. You are only meant to experience all that it has to offer. When you achieve the path of unconditional love and acceptance within yourself, you receive your true identity—the identity of the whole without separation. When you live your life in unison with your heart and mind connected, you move with the energies around you and need not force the hand of change, but allow it to draw to you the things that are necessary for spiritual growth. As you acknowledge and accept the existence of a higher force, you can reconnect back to this force in order to discover who you are. When you are silent within yourself, then you begin to see who you are and allow the unfolding of your true identity. You are a balanced spiritual being that only fluctuates when you let your emotional attachments control you.

Through your experiences, the world that you live in is the playground for the development of your physical, mental and spiritual growth. When you are no longer preoccupied with the need to survive and compete against yourself and with others, you are finally drawn back to the center of your spirit: the heart. When you deal with matters of the heart, you make yourself vulnerable to your spirit, which allows for further growth within your own spiritual development. It reminds you of who you are, what you are here to experience and what matters most: the vibration of love. From the moment a mother gives birth and holds her child in her arms, the vibration of love creates the connection from mother to infant, sibling to siblings, husband to wife, friend to friend, for generation after generations to come.

Only a handful of people are remembered for their achievements as decades, centuries and millennia pass by. Their contributions to the advancement of humanity best resonates their achievements within their time. The ones that have received the greatest acknowledgements, most respect, and have been most revered are the ones that shifted the consciousness of humanity. Those individuals taught love, respect, acceptance in all things, which is the same potential within you. They achieved their divinity by looking at the resistance within themselves, the resistance between being human and becoming spirit. The heart chakra connects you back to spirit, back to your heart and the energies that surround you. Here, you connect to the vibration of creation and the vibration of love. You have come here to experience the different degrees of giving and receiving love within yourself until you are able to detach from life's experiences and love the world. By empowering this vibration, you empower yourself with the desire to seek higher truths. That is the next step in consciousness development: seeking the spirit within you.

CHAPTER 8

THROAT
CHAKRA

T he fifth chakra body, also known as the throat chakra, is
located in the throat region. The vocal cords within your
throat give you the ability to speak and verbally communicate your thoughts, emotions, and creative expressions—what you
choose to express outwardly within your physical world. The throat
chakra represents your spirit's need to communicate energetically the
expression of truth within the thoughts and emotions that give rise
to self discovery. Your creative expression is the true nature within
your spiritual identity. Just as your voice is a means of communicating
through the creation of sound and vibrations, your spirit communicates through the vibration of energies that manifest your creativities.
The throat chakra allows you to further unfold your true spiritual
identity as you seek truth within you. As you connect to your spirit
on deeper levels of attunement, your spirit communicates back to

you through imaginative and intuitive thoughts, ideas and creativity. This is the unique spiritual identity that holds your innate gifts.

Courtnee, a young woman from Sacramento, California, was born into an unstable home environment. Her biological father had abandoned his six-month old daughter to the care of her alcoholic mother. Courtnee's formative years brought an influx of constant uncertainty. Attempting to cope with the fallout of a mentally-troubled mother who needed severe help and guidance of her own, Courtnee had the heavy burden of taking care of and raising herself. A sensitive child, she struggled with crushing bouts of depression, fear, confusion and a sense of guilt around her inherent strengths. This caused Courtnee to spend her teenage years in mental darkness and abuse. She traded the turmoil of her adolescence for the comfort and safety of solitude, which lead to severe substance abuse and multiple suicide attempts as she tried to find her own identity. Her broken body paid the price for her irreconcilable sadness.

In desperation, she looked for a way to express what she believed to be her true self in a world that, to her, was bereft of truth and full of contradiction and lies. A world where people praise you in person, but secretly laugh at you when you were gone. In seeking an outlet, Courtnee sought refuge in painting, singing and aerial acrobatics; she expressed herself through art. When she found herself unraveling mentally and emotionally following the devastating loss of one of her few childhood friends, Courtnee made a conscious choice to no longer be bound by a false sense of the world. This young woman chose to stop suffering, and embraced psychotherapy and meditation as vehicles that drove her to self-improvement. Slowly, these initial steps to finding her true self allowed her to see that true validation and real strength doesn't come from others; it comes from the self. The self is something you believe in, something you know to be true, and not something you are told. Courtnee finally believed herself to be worthy of love, worthy of accolades, and worthy of truth. She believes this now because of the strength of the human spirit, its ability to persevere, even during the most dire stresses and trials. Its power and beauty is unmasked in surrendering to the flows of the universe.

Once you begin to acknowledge and develop comfort within your own identity and the values of your own self-worth, you then direct your growth towards seeking what makes you unique within your own individuality. By knowing your forever evolving individuality, you understand the role of your expanding spirit within the universe. As you expand your intellect, you begin to further develop your own belief systems and acknowledge yourself and your own self-worth within that belief system. You begin to feel knowledgeable and comfortable in your own skin and with who you are. You begin to formulate ideas and truths with the knowledge that you have acquired. When you stand within this knowledge, you begin to seek and attract others of like mind and similar beliefs within your current consciousness resonation. Through social interaction and synchronicity, you are then able to attract your teachers, mentors and your students in order to help each other proceed along your chosen paths. What you may perceive as coincidence is, in actuality, the appointed time that you draw to you what you need when you are ready to listen and learn. Within the development of your fifth level of consciousness, your desire to seek for a higher truth is always met with the right teachings that meet your level of desire and intention.

Have you ever wanted to learn or know more about something, and then suddenly someone tells you about a book, a class, or a television show on the exact subject that you wanted to know more about? Have you ever felt stuck in your learning, whether personal, business, or spiritual, when suddenly a thought, a person, or a clear path opens up for you to follow? As the saying goes, "When the student is ready the master appears." When you have arrived at the fifth level of conscious development, you attract the proper guidance, teachers, or information that is necessary to help you further evolve in knowing your true self.

Sometimes the right of mastery is given to us by our peers. Usually a teacher must first gain the respect of his or her students; otherwise, a master is no more important than a stranger we have passed in the street. To most, we are only as important as others allow us to feel or as we believe ourselves to be as important. But true masters are able to resonate their own vibrations and truths from within themselves and do not seek the approval or recognition of others. Their frequency vibrations are simply felt when in their presence. It is most important to remember that we are all masters and students for one another within the experience we call life. We all have something to offer to others in the learning experience as we learn the many levels within ourselves. Although we may have different levels of knowledge and understanding; we can always be reminded of our own humility and continue to learn and share within each others' experiences as teachers and students of light.

To learn from the knowledge and experience of your teachers can help direct you further along your chosen path, allowing you to experience and unfold your own answers. You are capable of being your own true master, the best teacher for yourself. Teachers appear in your life to help you along the journey until you are able to support and master yourself. Anyone who claims to have the answers for someone else's path by way of his or her own path should be carefully scrutinized for their false intent. The teacher can only assist through guidance until the student outgrow the master's teachings and moves on to continue the journey to finding herself on her own unique path.

Your desire to seek higher truths and greater understanding of your own existence directs you along a path of learning more about you. With the desire to further learn, educate and improve yourself and your life, you begin to unfold a deeper understanding about who you are. As you empower yourself, you begin to deepen your desire for truth. When you know something to be true within you, you know it because you feel it. Within your knowing and feeling resides the energies of your own spiritual vibration that cannot be shaken until your truths and experiences further evolve. Have you ever told a story about your experiences and someone tells you that you're lying or that it was impossible or not true? Have you ever been told a story and didn't believe it until you had to experience it yourself? Have you ever had to defend your own truth? Sometimes in evoking or defending your truths, the emotional energies surrounding your truths shake you to the core.

All of the thoughts, actions and emotions that make up your whole being vibrate from the consciousness of your experiences, your attachments, and your truths at your present time. Through your physical actions and verbal communication, you project energies empowered by the emotion of your thoughts and judgments in the everyday choices of your life. Every word spoken, every action taken sets a vibrational intention that is projected forth as vibrational energy. Just like prayer or meditation, these are purposeful releases of your energies within your everyday acts and communications. In the same sense, your daily actions are also forces of communicative energy. From the instant that you think, speak or act, you send forth vibrations with your perceived acts or intentions in a form of positive or negative energy.

To understand the idea that you are simply energy resonating and attracting positive or negative energy helps to understand this same concept at the quantum mechanics level. You are made up of free-floating charged particles of free-flowing energy. Even if you are unable to comprehend or acknowledge this idea, you cannot deny that you are living and breathing charged particles transformed into human flesh. Every thought that you create manifests as an electrical impulse in your brain. This impulse is sent through your nervous system to perform the intended action or movement in your body. This releases or generates the electrical impulse in your body needed to perform such actions as movement, digestion, function and so on. In doing so, energy is generated and transferred from one form to another and is then emitted from your body in various forms.

Based on these principles, you can gather that electrical impulses are constantly running through your body in an effort to maintain a healthy living vehicle for the spirit to exist and utilize within the human experience. On an energetic level, your chakra bodies are energy centers that resonate the growth and development of your spiritual consciousness. Your meridian systems, based upon traditional acupuncture and Eastern medicine, are the pathways of positive and negative energies, carrying chi flow, spiritual energy, and communication to various parts of the human body. Therefore, you emit general baseline frequencies or vibrations that encompass your entire body. As a conglomerate, these energetic vibrations can be seen as your aura or etheric body. The auric field is the energy field in which you emit or display the vibrational communication of your spirit through your thoughts, actions and emotions based on your vibrational intentions. This is the basic premise on which you communicate and project your powers of intention into the universe. Through the vibration of your spirit, you manifest and attract positive and negative events within your life, vibrationally communicating with the energetic field of your surroundings.

The power of your creative or imaginative thought process initiates the growth and development of your intuitive communication with you and your spirit at lower levels of consciousness. As you raise your vibrations, you are able to access greater abilities that allow you to project your energies forward. As stated earlier, higher energies of good intentions resonate at a higher and faster frequency; therefore, it can nullify and void lower negative vibrations—growth versus decay. The more your life is connected to your own spirit, the higher the vibrations you can manifest.

Remember that you are connected to various aspects of your spirit at all times, dark and light, and you can choose to empower either end of the spectrum. How you choose to focus your beliefs and intentions outwardly can empower energies or entities outside of yourself, for any spirit or energy is an energy that exists when recognized. This is the balance of the universe. Until you can learn how to develop and empower your own energies of the spirit, you can sway toward the negative or positive vibrations within you equally, based upon judgments and the perceptions that you attach to within the energy field of your surroundings. At the physical level of your mental body, the ego directs the chaos of your emotions through the reception of your environment and your sense of perceived power and control. At higher levels of consciousness, the ego becomes the driving force of your wisdom, and your divinity comes forth and brings you back into balance by the vibration of your higher will.

As you reach the level of empowering yourself with conscious and directed thoughts, you enhance the level of your vibrations in whichever direction you choose. Whether you use visualization, mantras, affirmations, positive talk or even listening to others speak their wisdom, you are empowering your human spirit. You simply stimulate your vibrations based upon the tool you choose and become your own personal coach. When you have problems doing such things by yourself because your emotions have taken control of your self-esteem or self-worth, you may recruit outside sources to help redirect you or guide you back in the right direction. You may seek personal coaches, psychiatrists or even spiritual teachers. But the truth remains that you are your own source of true empowerment; you are the one to decide when to act or empower yourself to accept and change the direction that you choose. It is your mental body that ultimately decides consciously whether you choose to control or be controlled by your emotional body. When you master your mental mind and let go of your own false attachments and perceptions, you are able to empower yourself with your own abilities and remain silent and balanced within your own presence.

As you let go of the mental mind's need to control, you are able to connect to the higher vibrations or intuitive nature that communicates and creates your physical and spiritual needs. When you come from a point of humility and humbleness, you are a clean slate that can be utilized and molded to manifest your higher will and benefit the whole versus the self. You are able to start from a point of clarity by empowering a single focus versus a diluted display of confusion. Your mind is no longer confused about which direction to go. You are content in a single direction of advancing the spirit and the body in whatever direction is needed. You begin to raise the vibration of your own consciousness that aligns you closer to your spirit.

So how can you best raise your vibration to access higher levels of consciousness in yourself? How can you be in touch or closer to your spirit? How can you know and better understand truth? Have you tried to seek the answers to these questions and come away more confused or frustrated in your efforts? Have you studied and followed a number of different spiritual teachings that left you confused as to what is really the answer or is very vague in finding these answers?

Christianity has taught us to pray to "God" for guidance or in essence demand things that we don't already have in our lives, thus addressing a sense of "lack" within ourselves and within our lives. We are sending out the vibrations of our intentions into the universe with selfish direction of our intended want. Buddhism teaches us to sit and meditate by clearing the mind so that we may see and experience ourselves. If your intention is to clear the mind, then you allow for detachment from the outside world, but at the same time all you have is yourself at whatever level you may have entered. You detach from the world by clearing your mind but do not feed your energies from a source that is higher than your current level of consciousness.

Based upon your spiritual genetic makeup, if you continue this way, you progress at a toad's pace. If you agree that we are all part of the universal consciousness or come from a divine source, then consider what you could access if you direct your level of intention or devotion to the level of that higher vibration. By placing your mental intentions at a level that is higher than where you currently vibrate, you allow yourself to reconnect to that higher level of vibration and begin to reconnect back to your divine essence of being: the higher self.

When I first began my journey towards knowing God, I would use a combination of prayer and meditation. I would begin reading an intended piece of scripture from the Bible. I then sat in stillness. I would ask God, which I now know to be my higher self, to show me my path—or God's will for me here on this Earth—by asking myself, "What is my highest purpose and what was the reason I was placed here on this Earth? Show me your will for me." My intentions were pure and not of selfish or self-serving means. I asked for nothing but guidance and direction in whatever form it might manifest in my life for the higher good of all. My blind faith was my strength. The more frequently I repeated this practice, the more my own intentions were empowered and directly focused on raising my vibration and receiving the guidance that I asked for until my own life manifested before my eyes into this physical body. This provided direction and drew to me the right healers and teachers at the right time, when my own consciousness was ready. The union of the higher self and the lower self then became one; the entry into understanding and experiencing levels of enlightenment, awakening, heaven and inner peace began. This is simply the story of my own path, which demonstrates the power of our intentions manifested within the physical self.

Prayer is when we speak to "God, Buddha, Source," or what I like to refer to as the "higher self." How you choose to speak your words is very important with setting the intention of your desires. Meditation is when you listen. When you combine your intentions within meditation, you direct the power of your intentions, your spiritual energies, and guide it towards manifestation. The reality is that your spirit is not physical, tangible, and not human, and cannot be guided, defined, or interpreted by human consciousness. Therefore, seek your higher self from a point of humility and out of unconditional love and acceptance for all, no matter which religious or spiritual doctrine you choose to follow. Seek yourself. In finding yourself, you will find your higher self, that which is connected to universal consciousness and the divine. Raising your own vibration is the key to manifesting your life's path.

At this fifth level of consciousness, you are able to choose to live your life or become an unconscious victim of it. Until you have mastered the human consciousness and step into the presence of your higher consciousness, you can vacillate between the levels of survival and the need to control. You choose your limitations and the truths that you empower through your mental attachments. Observe your thoughts and beliefs, for it is easy to create mental or physical limitations within your physical and spiritual development. You can become limited to the physical world and its social laws of acceptance within the mental boundaries you choose to attach to and empower. To overcome mental limitations that reside within your level of desires, choose not to be limited by other people's beliefs and expectations. Learn to empower your own truth and the will of your spirit.

The power of your own beliefs can be much greater than what society conditions you to believe. Steve Prefontaine is considered to be one of the greatest American distance runners in history. Having been born with one leg significantly shorter than the other, Steve was told by numerous medical professionals, family members and friends to give up his dreams of becoming the fastest runner on Earth. However, he chose to empower his dreams. In the late sixties and early seventies, Steve had a remarkable college track record. He received seven NCAA titles in track and field and was the first to win four consecutive NCAA titles in the three-mile. He also held eight collegiate records. At the height of his running career, Steve held every American track and field record ranging from the 2,000 meter to the 10,000 meter. Steve's life ended on May 30, 1975 when a fatal car accident took his life at the early age of 24, but his legacy lived on. Steve Prefontaine lived by the belief that "To give anything less than your best is to sacrifice the gift."

The simple act of believing what you are told, what you can or cannot do, what you can or cannot become, has limited your own growth and has empowered separation amongst many people, races, and religions throughout the centuries. By consciously agreeing to believe in these social paradigms, you therefore work within the parameters given, which are dictated by man-made laws of mental limitation or mental control instead of universal truths of love, acceptance, and equality to evolve to your full potential.

We see these limiting perceptions taking place in social and religious groups, human and civil rights organizations, activist and protest groups, private and public organizations. Allowing yourself to be identified and labeled as someone separate, someone different, someone who is oppressed, judged, categorized, and defined a certain way gives you the perception of having more or less privileges than others around you. It provides you the excuse of existing under the limitations that define your human existence, devaluing and falsely empowering who you are within your own rights, gifts and talents. Enabling these implemented belief systems causes you to vacillate back and forth within the first five levels of human consciousness. Your perceived free will dictates the ego's control of the human mind that limits your spiritual identity. You empower false self-created illusions of separation, domination, survival, and resistive forces within you. You choose your life based upon the empowerment of your misdirected ego through your perceived control or lack thereof. It is you who chooses to use the force of creation versus the power of manifestation from the higher self. Force exposes you to resistance and can create mental roadblocks from your need to control within your physical illusion. The power of control can influence people, cities, countries, and nations to the brink of insanity and towards human cruelty if it goes unchecked.

Why is force a form of resistance? Force is the strength or power exerted upon an object. It is physical coercion or violence: *to use force to open the window; to use force on a person.* The amount of force needed to invoke movement needs to be greater than the energy force of the opposing force or individual. The energy within the opposing force is the resistance that pushes back against the force being imposed. When you force action, you manifest a reaction that is consequence-based. When someone yells at you, you yell back. When someone hits you, you hit back. When someone abuses you, you reject them. It is your innate survival defense mechanism that tells you to protect yourself as best you can. The lower your vibrations, the greater the reaction of consequence, creating the separation between perceived man and God. If you cannot govern yourself in the state of unconditional love and acceptance, you are treated and governed by a law of separation; you are taught that a higher power or force is your final judgment and entrance to heaven or nirvana. Until you have fully accepted yourself, you remain a child learning and growing within the life you have chosen to accept. It is simply a choice of accepting who you are and how you choose to live your life or become a victim to it. When higher consciousness is achieved, you are being guided and empowered by *you*, holding yourself to full responsibility for the way you choose to live your life, free from blame or victimization.

As you ascend the levels of consciousness, you receive greater insight and are given further knowledge and understanding as to who you are and where you come from. A feeling of belonging or connect-edness is the key to seeking and advancing the self. Until you reach a level of community, you see yourself as separate and act selfishly in return. The falsely empowered ego becomes your master and the God of your world, proclaiming itself as the ruler of your physical world and the physical self. With its self-proclaimed righteousness and self-devotion towards desire, the misdirected ego diverges and misleads your own innate knowledge and truths. Empowering the ego to the desires of your own selfish needs or wants creates separation within your spirit and therefore halts your spiritual growth. To live within the realms of unconditional love and abundance, you must learn to detach from the physical false reality of selfish desire and walk in your divine spiritual right. The path to your divinity is through you and you alone, not through worshipping the attachments of the physical world or an energy source beyond yourself.

If the principles are clear within all spiritual teachings and philosophies, it is perplexing that we create false interpretations within religions that create division among us and cause us to speak out against others. Society has created religions to be a collective false ego for the masses to generate and validate false reasons for our own self-destruction. The man-made self-created false ego is exemplified when countries fight over sacred lands in the name of religion or God. In the Bible, God and Master Jesus spoke of unconditional love: to not strike back, but offer the other cheek, to do unto others as you would like have done to you, to not covet. Yet all we see is the opposite, the formation of man's pride and the survival of the animalistic ego within nations. We see an empowered mass with a false premise—worshipping a false "God" for all the wrong reasons—and on a path towards forced control and self-destruction.

The whole purpose of spiritual teachings is to direct us in loving one another, even when others aren't able to see love before them. We help lift each other in order for all of us to stand in love. Life is the experience of learning the many faces of love and then being shown how to love in return—to love unconditionally. Whether you want to call it love, compassion, forgiveness, humility, they are all examples of the many layers of love within the human spirit. To show love in the face of anger, hatred, wrongness, prejudice, or pride is an opportunity to learn how to give and receive love. If you come from a divine vibration of unconditional love and acceptance, then the vibration of love and acceptance in the face of anything is what you truly are.

When you separate yourself from the higher will of your higher self, separating humanity from God, the unobtainable, you become what you reap, the vibration of your lower consciousness—animalistic survival. You become a child of a lesser God, ruling out of your lower level consciousness. This is the behavior and expression that creates wars, the destruction of our humanity and separation from God or universal consciousness. Becoming so prideful in your own ego is disrespectful not only to your chosen religion, but also to yourself both physically and spiritually. When you segregate or put down another's chosen path or spiritual teaching, you choose to live in separation. You become a victim to your false perception and fall under the law of your own chosen circumstance.

We procreate children in our own likeness. They are a part of us physically and spiritually and eventually will grow up to be adults like us. Similarly, the Bible states that "God" created humanity in our own likeness. So you therefore have the ability to empower yourself to grow into something greater: your higher self. You have the choice of how you want to live and perceive your life. You choose whether you want to grow or stand still. You are your own keeper until your physical life expires and you are returned to spirit form. It is your choice to take the next step, to consciously leave the womb of your human existence and step into your spiritual integration. This takes you one step closer to integrating the higher energies of your spirit into your physical life, becoming that which you are meant to be. In taking on the higher levels of responsibility and accountability within yourself, you begin to unlock innate spiritual gifts that allow you further access to spiritual learning and the ability to see and interact within the non-physical existence that surrounds you. In doing so, you gain greater knowledge, understanding, and wisdom that expands your experience so that all of us may benefit from the vibration of your own wisdom.

CHAPTER 9

THIRD EYE

The sixth chakra body, also known as the third eye, is located in the middle of your forehead or brow. As you raise the energy levels of your human vibration, you increase the energy of your spiritual body, which nurtures the development of your spiritual body. As light is able to pierce the darkness for you to see, the light of your spiritual body allows you to feel and see intuitively beyond your physical senses. The development of your psychic faculties allows you to further see and understand the physical and non-physical dimensions of existence that surround you. With this expanded vision, you begin to understand and self-reflect the origins of your spiritual existence and reason for physical existence. Self-reflection is the capacity of humans to exercise introspection and the willingness to learn more about your fundamental nature, purpose and essence. You begin to learn, interact, and utilize the information around you in preparation for receiving from your spirit further knowledge and information about you.

As you begin the journey toward your identity, individuality, and eventual totality of who you are, you initially learn through your experiences in the physical world and through your five physical senses—sight, sound, touch, smell and taste—that integrate the experience into knowledge. We know and see one another as we do because we vibrate at similar ranges of physical frequency. Of course, there are also things that we are not able to see due to different resonations of frequency, though they still exist, seen or unseen. As you become able to ascend and obtain higher levels of vibrations, you begin to gain access to your non-physical senses. These non-physical senses become an extension of your own physical attributes and knowledge, including the integration of using your own energies to interact with other levels of vibrations. This gives way to your second sight and intuitive abilities. It is not until you have mastered these senses, and made use of them to your fullest extent, that you are given new skills to augment and further develop your abilities. You can only work from your present place of learning and understanding until you are ready to learn the next step or ability.

As you begin your ascension into the higher vibrations and higher levels of consciousness, you begin to manifest your God-like or divine abilities—the ability to see and know all. Because few have reached these levels of higher consciousness, the descriptions of psychic abilities and skills often sound fantastical, incomprehensible, paranormal, or bizarre. Therefore, it is important to remain open and without mental boundaries or judgment (such as doubts or assumptions), in order to access these higher levels. At the sixth level of consciousness development, just as if you opened your eyes for the first time, you begin to see your life in a different way: through your third eye, the etheric eye that allows you to see intuitively the non-physical dimensions that exist all around you. The more open and unhindered you are, the more you can integrate your perception and communicate on a physical and non-physical level. This may initially come in the form of intuition, visions, moving and nonmoving images, channeling or even seeing and communicating with spiritual beings. As you learn how to utilize your non-physical attributes, you must re-learn how to interpret and understand the information you are given with your newly expanded sixth sense. Just like a newborn that opens its eyes for the first time to see strange new images and colors that were different from the warmth and darkness of its mother's womb, so will you need to adapt and integrate the new undefined images of the non-physical world with your current knowledge and understanding. This learning is left to your own trial and error of interpretations until you master the knowledge and understanding of the communication.

For some, psychic abilities and gifts are already active and in place since birth. Depending upon the nurturing, development and growth of these abilities, people born with psychic gifts can advance and strengthen their abilities, similar to how you attended school to advance your intellect through education and then utilized that knowledge in conjunction with your adult life experiences. For some, these gifts are suppressed, because they are born into environments that judge and label them as evil or bad. And for others still, the development of psychic abilities is still ahead on their journey towards spiritual evolvement. The vibration utilized in manifesting these gifts is similar to the vibrations used in the connection between a newborn and its mother or the intuitive feeling that one gets when someone close to them is suffering or in danger. We all have a degree of psychic ability that we access on various levels of consciousness. You develop your psychic skills when you advance your conscious awareness in the greater vision that surrounds you. Psychic abilities are merely tools that you access for further understanding and development of your higher consciousness.

With the advancement of our intellect and the raising of our vibration as a whole society, we are also expanding the consciousness of future populations. This expansion allows for the nurturing of more and more gifted children to be birthed into the world, where they are not shunned or rejected but can utilize their psychic gifts from birth and remain connected to the astral or non-physical realms. With these gifts, some can remember times before they entered their bodies and have knowledge of previous lives. Depending upon the level of their parents' psychic heritage, they can enter into their physical bodies at various levels of vibration and ability.

Perhaps you have heard of the "Indigo Children," who vibrate an indigo color in their auric energy field, the same chakra color of the third eye. Some of you may have come across the rarer, higher resonating "Crystal Children." These children have immensely beautiful auras of gold or white light and hold a multitude of psychic gifts that seem miraculous to us. All of these children are rare and usually a mystery to current scientific or psychic knowledge and research. These higher vibrating children are sometimes mistaken for godly reincarnates due to their abilities. The reality is that they are a reflection of the actual capability within all of us. These individuals are simply able to descend their higher vibrations of their spirit into their physical bodies, a journey that is obtainable by all who are willing to follow their own paths toward seeking themselves.

The higher you are able to vibrate, the higher you can connect to different levels of your own spiritual expression. As you ascend towards your higher self, you descend and integrate your divine intelligence and spiritual abilities into your physical body. Once you have prepared your mind and your body to hold higher vibrations, then it is only a matter of time before your divine gifts manifest into the physical body. As you are better able to hold your higher vibrations, you become increasingly able to utilize your gifts within your everyday life. Your abilities develop over time the more you utilize them, because they become a part of your own senses within the physical body, just like your ability to taste the nuances of a food improves the more you eat it.

When your spiritual gifts are unlocked, they remain with you. However, when you choose to resonate at lower levels of consciousness for long periods of time through your everyday thoughts, choices and actions, you begin to lower the level of your own vibration and run the risk of having to reacquire your abilities or gifts. These gifts require a certain level of practice in order to be utilized, so you must once again raise the level of your vibration back to the level of access. Just like when you feel sick with a fever, you don't have the same energy to perform the regular daily activities, so rest is needed to rejuvenate your body back to good health and good function. The greater the gifts received, the harder it is to maintain its vibration based upon your choices within your everyday social interaction within your environment. Therefore, you must occasionally clear or recheck yourself to make sure you remain open and connected to your higher consciousness and not bound to your lower consciousness and physical desires.

You vacillate up and down your levels of consciousness depending on how you interact in your everyday life. As you let go of mental barriers and focus on raising and expanding your level of consciousness, you force your vibrations to expand outside of your own comfort level and allow for increases in your vibrations. You can achieve this through setting your intentions within your meditations as well as learning and practicing things that are utilized at higher levels of understanding. Detachment, prayer, meditation, forgiveness, compassion—these are teachings within all religions that remind you to be at peace with yourself and not at war with the outside world. The mental mind is your only barrier. As you break the barriers within your mind, you are able to activate the abilities of your spiritual body as well as access other parts of your brain. With the activation of higher levels of consciousness, you gain access to new information and ideas that are not taught in a physical medium, but from the vibration of universal truth.

Until we are able to break through the mental boundaries that we place upon ourselves, we remain infantile in spirit and become trapped within the illusion of the physical existence. The activation of your third eye begins the non-physical development of your spiritual growth and your exposure and interaction to the different dimensions within the astral realm. As you further use your psychic abilities beyond simple vision and interpretation, you may then choose to develop other areas of psychic communication through projection, which can be demonstrated in the form of telepathy or channeling internal communications. We become so used to our own internal dialogue that we tend to keep asking ourselves, "Is this real or is this all just in my head?" The explanation that I tend to relay to the person who has acquired their newly psychic gift is that your imagination doesn't talk back to you unless you put the words in its mouth. Only psychic communication can do that. As you increase your vibrations, you can eventually acquire the ability to transcend the physical body and project the spiritual body for astral travel, or project your vision into various places, known as remote viewing.

There can sometimes be confusion or a discrepancy of psychic communication between the internal voice of a split personality or fractured fragment within the spirit. Where do you draw the line to differentiate between psychic communication and the internal voice of a split personality? An internal voice or internal noise, depending on what level of consciousness you choose to resonate at, is a fragmented reflection of yourself that you empower or a fragment of your spiritual self penetrating through your current level of consciousness. When you remain bound in your lower level resonations such as anger, depression, feelings of rejection or low self-worth, suicidal tendencies or any negative expression, you harness and expand that lower level of vibration. With enough vibrational stimulation, a lower fragment of the spirit can empower itself to hijack your own vibrational energy and separate itself from the spiritual body. The empowered fragment becomes separated or an individual frequency within the whole frequency of the spirit, what psychiatrists like to call split personalities, but which is really a separated lower spiritual fragment.

Lower levels of consciousness are all about survival and self-preservation. These lower level fragments may, as cost of self-survival, ask you to do harmful things to yourself or someone else. These thoughts and actions generate more and more low level frequencies to further their own survival. When empowered, this split of the animalistic ego consciousness becomes a constant and menacing force that tries to control and rule the physical self like an outsider looking in. Whereas before you were in control in the development of all of your spiritual fragments, you are now in control only of your carnal thoughts. When separated and empowered, the vibrational fragment becomes its own identity and can wreak havoc on the already weakened and feeble mind that you chose to empower through your negative expression. This in effect is simply empowering a negative expression of one of your archetypes, one of many that you hold within the structural formation of the spirit representing the full spectrum of positive and negative expressions.

When you focus your intentions to your higher will, you connect to higher levels of consciousness and improve guidance within your intuition. At the level of the higher will, there is no judgment of a negative or harmful nature. When you connect to higher consciousness, you are directed from a place of balance, acceptance and abundance for you and everyone around you. You choose the direction you want to take because you are in control of your mental thoughts and the actions of your physical body. Of course, the "higher" road is ideal or recommended, but ultimately we choose our experiences for our lives and teach ourselves our own lessons through the choices of our experiences. For some, the higher road is the ideal choice to follow, but you must keep in mind that the desires of a falsely empowered ego can play a significant part in redirecting you momentarily off the beaten path of the self. Even though you may clearly see what the right choice is for yourself, sometimes you still choose to continue to make wrong decisions. These usually stem from moments of selfishness or emotional attachment to your past that haven't been cleared from the spirit.

We often see this when a relationship or partnership has ended, yet we battle against the warning signs to try to prolong something that was meant to end. Our own personal ego tells us that "me" can make it work because "me" is strong, "me" can't fail or be the cause of failure. "Me" still needs to feed who is most important: "me," the falsely empowered ego of our own selfish desires, which translates to our own fear of the unknown. We are like children who, when told they can't have candy, TV, or other wants that are not healthy in excess, end up wanting them even more. Children do not see their parents' wisdom. They only see that their fun time is being taken away. They ask, "What about me?" When you allow yourself to choose from lack of wisdom, you expose yourself to further consequence and destruction.

When you choose to remain at lower levels of consciousness, you tend to believe that what you see is what you get, what you do is what you create. You believe that everything in this world is orchestrated by what you and other people do by force. You believe that you create your world based on your actions and achievements. This is true at the lower levels of survival, based on the interactions between people at the same level of consciousness. A person's vibration may attract like vibrations and therefore create a mass conglomeration. Just as you can choose a higher vibration at which to resonate, you can choose a lower vibration at will. You seek at the level of your vibrations and attract at the same level, because of familiarity and like mind.

Your community conveys a general consciousness resonation, because the overall level of consciousness holds a median level of conscious vibration that affects the growth and development of the people within it. So as a participant within the community of humanity, it is your responsibility to help others raise their own vibrations in order to bring balance and harmony to the whole. This is not necessarily done by trying to save everyone you meet or by doing as many good deeds as you can. Savior syndrome is just as ineffective and identity-dependant as someone who chooses to be a victim (martyr syndrome). Saviors feed their dependency on the approval of other people's energies for the empowerment of their own egos. Like narcissists and people with low self-esteem, both need the stimulation of constant attention. Saviors constantly need other people's approval to fulfill a sense of lack within the self. The question becomes, how do you really serve your community? By simply holding your own level of vibration, you hold or raise the vibration for your community. By seeking higher vibrations, you raise the vibrations for you and your community.

The higher you vibrate, the more you can affect lower vibrations. You also help raise the vibration of the world that you live in, just by being you. It abides by the same law as osmosis—the passage of a liquid from an area of high concentration through a semi-permeable membrane to an area of low concentration. Eventually, a new equilibrium is achieved.

After twenty seven years in prison, Nelson Mandela, a black man within a white separatist nation, was able to help end apartheid in South Africa. Mandela was sentenced to life in prison for his leadership role in the African National Congress (ANC). During nearly three decades he spent in prison, he came to represent the struggle against apartheid and became an icon for freedom and equality. Most of his confinement was spent in a small cell on Robben Island. Political prisoners were isolated from the rest of the inmates. He was allowed one visitor and one censored letter every six months. Despite his suffering, he consistently refused to compromise his personal and political beliefs in exchange for freedom. When finally released in 1990, Mandela resumed his leadership of the ANC and directed the party in the negotiations that led to the country's first multi-racial elections. He received the Nobel Peace Price for his leadership in 2003. In 2004, Nelson Mandela became the first democratically elected State President of South Africa. It was his policies of reconciliation and negotiation that eventually led to the end of apartheid.

The reality is everything you do vibrationally affects everything around you. Simply being who you are—your highest potential—and holding the vibrations of your own energies are the best ways to affect your environment. Scripture says Master Jesus and Master Buddha's aura, or presence, could be seen and felt from miles away. Their vibrations mirrored the level of their consciousness and freedom from attachment to the physical world of the illusionary self. They resonated at their highest expression of divine vibration, their higher self in their physical bodies. The power of their consciousness had a lasting impact for generations afterward.

What motivates us to seek the next level of vibration past our human consciousness? When you can see beyond the illusion or identification to the physical world, you come to the understanding that you are more than your physical body and your attachments to your experiences. There is more to you than meets your physical eyes. When you advance to levels of consciousness past the physical self, past human consciousness, you once again become a student to the universe. You choose how to partake in its vibrations. You begin the journey with detachment from the physical world and false desires of the self. You see that you are part of a grander vision and that your sense of "me" is an incomplete view of who you actually are. You begin the journey towards higher will, community, and selflessness.

Realize that you were part of a greater vibration before entering your physical body. As you connect back to this higher source, you remember and receive what was lost before entering your physical body. As you grow spiritually within your physical body, you open the ability to acknowledge spiritual gifts that are abundant within you. The higher you are able to vibrate, the greater the gifts received, and as it is said, "With great power comes great responsibility." You can, however, only hold this responsibility when you hold your own accountability and choose not to reference blame elsewhere to a source outside yourself. In the end, you make your own decisions and direct your desired outcomes. You decide how to utilize your life to experience yourself and your own divinity.

The perception of the self is contained within the reality in which you create your mental boundaries. If you choose to believe that your physical life—what you do, how you think—is created in what is tangible or physical, then you are governed by the laws and limitations of your physical world. To believe in a greater power, a greater source, or even God, as a source that assists you in life gives you the belief of added strength. However, with the belief that something greater is out there watching over you and helping every step of the way, you remain a child who is governed. If instead you align with your spirit, the part of you that comes from infinite power and creation, then you are governed by your true self and the wisdom that comes with the vibration of the universe. You are able to grow beyond your spiritual childhood into the adulthood of your full potential of divine spirit. Whatever level you choose to abide by, you are governed until you are able to govern yourself. You are governed by the level of consciousness in which you choose to live. Ultimately you decide your own destiny, karmic lessons, or fate, based simply upon your own level of consciousness. You understand that you choose what to experience in each lifetime.

Each level of consciousness that you experience and attach to holds a series of karmic lessons to experience, each based on the karmic vibration of your past and past lives at each level. You ascend past these lessons when you are able to step up to take on a new path. There exists a new set of lessons at each level of consciousness that you experience during the ascension of consciousness within the lower self—the first seven chakra bodies. You can always choose to step back into karmic lessons and relearn them when you vacillate or revert back to lower levels of consciousness. The higher you are able to vibrate, the fewer lessons you need to learn, until you become a witness to your own manifestation. You cannot want what you already have, therefore want or lack within yourself only happens when you do not acknowledge the master within you. The choice is up to you for how you want to experience your own life. You can decide what kind of world you want to experience. It is free for the taking. It all depends on what road you choose to follow. You are the "experiencer" of your physical existence until you become the master of your spiritual destiny. In order to master yourself, you must master your ability to learn, communicate, and interact within the physical and non-physical dimensions of your existence. When you are able to master your spiritual gifts, you can learn to directly receive from your higher self and receive the wisdom of your true spirit.

CHAPTER 10

CROWN
CHAKRA

The seventh chakra body, also known as the crown chakra, is located at the top of the head and connects you to the consciousness of your spiritual awareness. It is the chakra which integrates all the chakra bodies with their respective qualities known as Universal Identity. This level of development contains the final integration of your lower self in the conscious evolution of your human awareness. It allows you to learn and experience yourself with universal and dimensional perspective. Just as your root chakra grounds and connects your spirit to Mother Earth and your physical life, the crown is the vortex to your higher self through the doorway to the many levels of enlightenment. It is where you receive knowledge from your higher self, allowing for the awakening of your divine spirit within the physical existence.

Once you've mastered your physical and spiritual abilities by learning how to decipher and utilize the various gifts and talents that await within you, you begin to see life a little more clearly. You see that the spiritual world mirrors the physical world in many ways. The astral or non-physical planes of existence are merely an extension of your own world. The spiritual beings that occupy it are only as mystical or as powerful as you empower them to be. Therefore, there are many beings at various levels of abilities, wisdom and consciousness similar to the diversity displayed within our physical world. Interacting and communicating at the astral level is not the end result of spiritual advancement. Being psychic at any level is only an extension of the senses in which your energetic body receives information from the energy field of your surroundings. When you understand that you are more than that of your physical existence, then you begin the journey toward reconnecting back to your higher self. When you are able to assemble your spiritual body, uniting your masculine and feminine parts as well as your spiritual fragments that were separated when you descended into your physical body, then you finally come to know what it is to be whole. To know and understand the spirit is to know and understand the spirit's makeup in order to unionize the spirit with the physical self. Your end goal is to become whole from within and awaken to your own light.

You were birthed of divine creation from your divine vibration. This same vibration that you came from holds the balance of creation and the inception of the universe. Before, we labeled this God. In reference to present perceptions, you are divinely connected to your higher self and your own divinity. At this level, "God" is understood and redefined as a family of light beings, or what some may refer to as the "Circle of Light." Human interpretations and current social control have separated divinity from our personal existence, causing us to seek outside of ourselves, causing us to seek a false God. But, in fact, we were and still are a part of what many refer to as God within our spirit, within our vibration. The same universal vibration, from which we originated, helps hold the balance of the universe and the world that we live and create within. Before you entered your body, you were part of universal consciousness. When you leave your physical body, you reabsorb back into this vibrational spiritual form and back to universal consciousness. You are a crucial part of everything that has ever been created, because you come from the same source.

As an individual spiritual being, you are part of a whole vibration and every part of this vibration has its own purpose. Your spirit has a purpose in the genetic makeup of universal consciousness. You have a specific purpose that allows for balance, structure, and flow of universal vibrations to exist. Like bricks, wood, nails, and mortar without a blueprint or plan, we would all just be a pile of separated parts. Separated, we remain limited in expressing our collective potential, but unified and interwoven together, we are a part of the creative intelligence that shapes and molds itself into infinite possibilities. As unique spiritual beings, we all have our purpose in the genetic makeup of universal consciousness, light and dark, which gives rise to balance, structure and flow. Realizing that you are a part of this divine vibration allows you to spiritually reconnect back to the family that makes up "God."

Your higher self is the highest vibration or expression that is a part of your divine essence of being, the part of you that is connected to universal consciousness. In essence, when you pray to God, you pray to the highest part of yourself. This is the part of you that is connected to the family known as God. When you call upon your deepest inner strengths, you touch the inner core of your spirit's vibration that reconnects back to your highest vibrations of your divine expression. When you enter through the doorway to knowing your higher self, you begin to open up your psychic gifts that allow you to learn, utilize and control your energetic body. Your higher source of consciousness and energy is all you need. As you ascend the ladder of consciousness, you may work with spiritual guides, beings or teachers in order to help you progress; this is part of your family that you attract vibrationally. However, without knowledge, experience and discernment, know that when you empower non-physical beings outside yourself, you lessen your own vibrations and lessen the strength of your own vibration. Your true guides, whether physical or non-physical, are here to teach and not control you or your life. Any teacher is only there to help guide you, not to be your source. The first commandment in Exodus 20:3 states, "You shall have no other Gods before me." This reminds you to be true to *you*, to believe and trust in yourself, and not to empower false things, false beings and false gods of the outside world. With this in mind, you can increase and enhance your own vibrations and trust in your personal higher consciousness without relying on outside forces or beings for your own strength, whether physical or non-physical. Understanding this principle allows deeper understanding towards awakening and obtaining levels of enlightenment within your spiritual self.

As you initially open your crown chakra to receive your higher intelligence, you become more sensitive to the energies around you. You may begin to feel different sensations in your body such as warmth, tingling, waves of energy or sensitivity to the higher vibrations of your surroundings or the energies of the people around you. You begin to further develop your third eye in order to access higher levels or other dimensions in order to increase your knowledge and awareness of universal consciousness. Colors of the chakra bodies, what you see with your psychic vision, or what you see when you close your eyes, may represent the higher energies that you are working with. You are receiving or communicating what you need to work on to further enhance your physical or spiritual development. When you learn to better understand and control the use of your psychic abilities, you may begin to see visions in the form of images similar to a photograph or a split second thought in your mind's eye. You may regard this at first as part of your imagination or your mind playing tricks on you, but the more you understand and utilize this information, the more you can interact and commune with your higher intelligence and trans-late it into your own wisdom and intuition. Other forms of psychic development may begin to manifest as brief moving pictures similar to your thoughts or your dreams, which may last for a few seconds or even longer, depending upon how well you are able to hold this level of vibration. As your abilities become more engrained within your physical body, you can remain present and aware when you choose to access the astral realms while deciphering your higher intelligence. These are controlled powers given to those who have mastered their psychic abilities.

Psychic development can also come in the form of channeling, where many psychics allow their bodies to be utilized as a funnel for other beings to speak and communicate through. Psychic channeling can be dangerous if you are unaware of your abilities or do not have control of your psychic gifts. Remember that not all beings in the astral realm are necessarily smarter or wiser than those in the terrestrial realm of our physical world. Astral beings are simply not bound by physical bodies and have full control of their energetic bodies and gifts. Some lower entities need the empowerment of your attention or awareness in order to thrive and exist within certain dimensions. If you allow anything or anyone to channel through you and give them full control of your body, you can expose yourself to deception, false information, or even lose control of your body. This can be seen in rare cases of demonic possession. To allow oneself to be an open channel gives rise to uncertainty. Just as you have the ability to lie or give false representation, so do beings in the astral realm. People new to their psychic abilities and not yet trained or experienced to its understanding or control can be easily fooled or manipulated. With channeling, it is important to be able to discern what is being received from the astral realm.

As stated before, you are vibrationally connected and are a part of everything energetically. Therefore, you are part of universal consciousness at some level or degree. How well you are able to understand and utilize your psychic senses will depend on the level of consciousness in which you open your psychic abilities. Most psychics are content to rely on "spiritual guides" and attach to their presence or being, but similar to how you advance in your schooling, changing classes and teachers in order to learn more advanced teachings, so does this premise relate in the development of your psychic abilities. When students have surpassed the teacher or guides and learned all that they can, it is time to advance to the next level for growth within the development of the spirit. This process repeats itself through the realms of higher consciousness, until you have reached the true mastery of yourself and can reconnect back to your higher self in order to further expand your conscious awareness.

What happens with mastery of psychic abilities? When you come full circle in the development and control of your psychic abilities, then you come to the level of non-separation between the psychic world and the physical world. You can act and communicate openly and freely within the physical and astral realm. At this level of control and understanding of your spiritual abilities, you can see, talk and relay information to non-physical beings just as if you were talking to the person next to you. You begin to see life and the universe for what it is: union in its entirety. There is no separation; therefore, there is no death or discontinuation in your life or the lives of others. The human experience we create for ourselves here on Earth is a playground created for our own learning through the illusions of our experiences. However, this world around you is not the complete reality, but only a vehicle to learn and grow from physical experiences into the completeness of your true self.

Of course achieving this totality of awareness is much easier said than done. It is hard to relate to such a thought or idea when the majority of us do not have the need or want to experience such understanding and ability. For most people, their intention in the physical world is based both upon how they interact and control the outlook of their lives and the relationships and experiences that they create within their immediate surroundings, perceived within the boundaries of their own mental minds. In other words, when you attach to what you see, hear, feel, taste and touch, it is only the given experience of the physical body which is inputted into your mental mind. The knowledge of the spiritual body is based upon your own desire to know and understand more of yourself. Accessing this higher knowledge begins with detachment from the physical world, the physical self, and the mental mind. You learn to not identify who you are with what surrounds you. It has everything to do with how you expend your focus and energy. Whether it is money, cars, houses, a better job or even another person's interest, people often use their human attributes to attach to their wants and desires. Then they find a way to obtain the intended goal. The energy projected outwardly to achieve these physical and emotional desires is the same energy that you use to manifest your spiritual self when redirected inward. You can use these same energies that you apply to external goals and redirect them internally to your spiritual goals.

Begin by setting forth your spiritual goals, intentions, or desires in the form of meditation or prayer. Whether you verbalize your intentions out loud or through your thoughts, it is the level of intensity and devotion of your desire that empowers your vibrations and manifest them into your physical existence. How much do you really want to know your true self? Is it a burning desire? Is it pure intent? How much do you want to evolve and grow? It is in the knowing, the feeling, that allows you to attract or manifest your desired outcome at the appropriate level of consciousness within you. As you send out your thoughts and intentions, you project your vibration to various levels within your own consciousness. The level that you perceive your own consciousness will resonate back the level of truth and understanding that you empower or believe to be your own limitation. Everyone may want to better or improve his or her life, but for what reason? Is it for self gain, identity, or survival? Or is it for a greater truth, a greater purpose that leads you down the path of learning unconditional love? The power of unlimited potential, unlimited possibilities, unlimited presence is found within the unconditional love and acceptance of the spirit, and not in the forced creation of the mental mind.

Most people want only what they see with the physical mind's eye and only consider achieving what is within their grasp. This is the way we are educated within our social paradigm. It's why most people only achieve what they think is possible by the examples of others around them. And then there are the few who dare to dream beyond the norm, beyond what most can conceive of. Your intentions enable you to create actions to acquire what you may desire or want to achieve. You can run circles around your daily physical life, yet spend little time attending, nourishing and developing your spiritual life. When people do choose to spend time on their spiritual development, it is usually directed toward learning and understanding a form or path outside of the self. Whether through religion, philosophy, church, monasteries, or classes, you are continually directed in focusing your energies to achieve and support forces that are outside of you. When you realize that you are connected and part of a greater experience, you can begin taking steps to advance your spiritual self from within. When the physical world has exhausted all of its bells and whistles that distract the mental mind and ego, you will come to realize that you are responsible for your own happiness. This is when you finally begin the journey inward towards finding your true self.

The fewer mental boundaries that you have to cross, the faster you can ascend the levels of your own consciousness. The energy, time and focus that you give to your spiritual efforts affect the rate at which you can manifest your spiritual gifts, access your higher self and evolve your spirit. Most people cannot learn calculus within a day, week or month, but must take years to grasp the teaching in their entirety. Little time spent is little effect received in the development of your own spirituality. You begin with the building blocks of understanding and then add to them little by little until you obtain deeper understanding to why you went through the process. As you take on the different levels of yourself, you push the ceiling of your understanding until there is nothing left to push—save a window to look through and eventually to climb out of. You find that you've climbed out of your own self-created mental box called the physical existence.

As you raise your levels of consciousness, you raise your human vibration. In her book, *Infinite Mind,* Dr. Valerie Hunt takes a scientific look at the chakra colors in relation to the human vibration. Using an aura reader, Dr. Hunt finds that the average human vibration resonates between 200 to 600 Hertz (Hz) in relation to the charka colors of the human energy fields. In order to achieve psychic chakra frequencies, you have to reach 700-800 Hz in order to enter the chakra colors of the sixth (high blue – 700 Hz) and seventh chakras (violet – 800 Hz). Aura colors of cream was measured at 1,000 Hz and white measured at 1,100 Hz, which represents divine light or guidance. Psychic frequency has been shown to be measured at 7.8 cycles per second (c/s) in brain wave studies. Relating hertz levels as frequency, in correlation to the chakra bodies, the resonation of human consciousness stops at 600 Hz, just below the sixth chakra body.

Increasing human frequency to the levels of 700-800 Hz allows us to access higher levels of consciousness within our spiritual development. This allows us the ability to see into the non-physical realms of existence. The fifth chakra body is the level of seeking truth within the level of human intelligence. Psychic or meditative frequency is measured at a narrow bandwidth of 700-800 Hz or 7.8 c/s. The seventh chakra body allows you to receive from a higher power, a higher source, and a higher level of intelligence within your higher consciousness. By relating the human vibration to human consciousness and the chakra bodies, you can see that in terms of the vibrational frequency, the human consciousness of human interpretation and reasoning resonates between 200 to 600 Hz, just below psychic frequency. Psychic and meditative frequencies resonate between 700 – 800 Hz, between the third eye and the crown chakra, the place of receiving your higher intelligence, and the doorway to the levels of enlightenment within the physical body.

Similarly, in Dr. David Hawkins' book, *Power vs. Force,* he evaluates consciousness development through a system of measurement based on applied kinesiology. If we relate spiritual conscious development to Dr. Hawkins' map of consciousness, 200 on his measurable scale is the consciousness level that separates good from bad, positive from negative. Comparing Dr. Hawkins' findings to the chakra system, we notice that between the second and third chakras human behavior changes from survival and lack to want and the development of power with our intentions. Dr. Hawkins also notes that 700 to 1000 on his measurable scale are levels of enlightenment or higher consciousness, the seventh chakra and up. So what if someone was able to calibrate past 7.8 c/s? When my human frequency was being tested, I was told that Albert Einstein calibrated at 1500 Hz. How do revolutionary ideas come about? The concepts of his special theory of relativity came to Einstein in his daydreams before he actually developed the theoretical formulas for relativity. Was Einstein able to tap into higher consciousness frequencies to bring forth the theory of relativity? Einstein completely changed the way we understand gravity and the speed of light. His work allowed other scientists to challenge his theories, paving the way for quantum physics. Out of these two radical theories, String Theory and M Theory were birthed, which today further aids in the understanding of the face and intelligence of God. Science is now bringing us even closer to our own truth and understanding of where we come from.

As you ascend past the psychic frequency, you continue to raise the levels of your vibration to greater depths of consciousness and open doors to increasingly advanced knowledge and understanding of the universe within yourself. The higher you are able to resonate, the better you are able to connect to greater levels of universal energies. Think of how dogs can hear frequencies far higher than humans. A dog is able to gain more knowledge of its surroundings than you or I could ever physically hear. When you develop your psychic senses, in relation to your increased spiritual awareness, you can similarly access information that you cannot currently see or hear. As stated earlier, universal consciousness is the oldest and greatest vibration that has ever existed and holds together the glue of universal energies and its matter. At birth, as you separated from this vibration, you descended your spiritual body into your physical body. Your spirit lowered its higher, faster moving vibration through dispersion, in order to exist within the physical body. In the descent, you detached from parts of your higher intelligence by lowering your spiritual vibration to exist in physical form. As you increase your human vibration, you eventually reconnect back to your spirit as you raise your energetic vibration on the journey back to your true self. This doesn't mean that you have ever lost any part of your spiritual being; your journey back towards spirit becomes a matter of reconnecting the spiritual body that has been dispersed within the physical body. Through ascending your own levels of consciousness, raising the level of your vibration, you have the ability to unlock the innate spiritual gifts within your physical body. Yet remember, that which is granted to you comes to fruition by your own efforts and no one else's.

When you focus your energies somewhere other than on yourself, you seek and empower another person's truth, causing you to move further away from finding and opening the truths that exist within you. Blindly following another's belief or path causes you to run into failure or complacency. You lower the level of vibration within yourself when seeking someone else's path to the self. Most people choose to believe and empower something other than themselves, because it removes the responsibility of achieving their desired intention. It is easier to follow life with another person's set of rules, values and teachings. Then you can say that you tried your best and it is okay to fail, because you are not them. It is easy to not be responsible for the greater, for one's personal self, not realizing that there exists a spiritual journey that leads to infinite possibilities. If you never accept the greatness within your true self, then you remain blissfully ignorant in seeking outside yourself, in awe of other things and other beings. You can never know the great potential that lies within the self when you remain trapped within the rules and restrictions of human interpretations, of what is truth and what is false. It requires courage and great leaps of faith, yet the rewards of trusting in your personal truths are infinite.

Consider the paradoxes that exist in conventional teachings. Why would an unconditionally loving God label his followers as sinners or rule them through judgment? Unconditional means without exception, without restriction and without condition, of the self and of you. Empowering these beliefs only allows for limitations with your spiritual evolvement. Giving away your power to those whom you have empowered in your life allows them to control and limit you of your growth and potential. Over the millennia, the word *sin* has been manipulated as a means to label, rule, judge, and control others. Any deviation from the norm was considered to be sinful or lack of good behavior. Sin now correlates to being bad or being uncontrollable. If you limit your experiences based on someone else's belief of what is considered to be correct, you limit your path towards achieving higher consciousness within yourself. The only misdirection is to move away from your true self, and even that path will eventually lead you back to you. It is simply a longer road with more lessons. Without knowledge or experience of totality, you delay the growth and development of your own divinity.

If you consider that freedom from the mind, thus rejection of the mind, is the doorway to enlightenment, then freedom from the mind is no better than choosing not to exist or experience the self. Do not seek to gain freedom or asylum from your mind. Rather, find the freedom through observing and detaching from the mind. Freedom is found through the enjoyment and unconditional acceptance of the learning experience without attaching to it adversely, as this would inhibit and stall growth of the self. You came into this world with a purpose to fulfill and you leave it with a measure of yourself. At the end of your physical life, how will you answer these questions: How did I do? What did I do? And how did it impact me and the world around me?

If you spend most of your life seeking and never seeing, then you have accomplished only a fraction of your own potential. There is religion and philosophy for those who need a crutch to support them until they are willing to follow the self. It is your own sense of lack and unworthiness within you that creates the sense of need that stands in the way of finding your divinity. There are many roads and many forms of travel from point A to point B. You will eventually arrive at the destination given the means and determination. The end goal is to get there on your own terms, through your own experiences. There is no right or wrong way but the judgment within your own self-created limitations. Starting from your intentions and actions, begin to form and create direction within yourself to manifest the intended path or goal. I urge you to take the first step in empowering and believing in yourself so that some day you may find yourself and see who you really are, perhaps for the first time in what might seem to be a long time.

Once you are able to access your higher intelligence from your own divinity, your higher self, you begin to clearly understand the purpose for each chakra body within the development of your physical-spiritual consciousness. The integration of each of these levels of consciousness allows for balance and unity of your spirit to exist within the lower seven chakra system, the lower self that makes up the physical existence. By understanding the union of your spiritual fragments, you gain perspective of your universal identity within the makeup of universal consciousness. The union of your spirit and creation is found within the summation of the fragments that makes up the whole of consciousness and the reason why you came here: to experience. At the doorway of your higher conscious, you leave behind your seeking and enter into understanding. Your vibrational awareness unites your individual consciousness with the universal consciousness, and its universal frequency of knowledge and existence. As your human consciousness is united with your spiritual consciousness, you awaken to the level of awareness of the collective consciousness as a whole. Here, you finally understand what it means to be whole.

Summary of Chakras

1. Root Chakra – Survivalist Identity / Animalistic Ego

2. Sacral Chakra – Emotional Identity / Desire, Emotional Body

3. Solar Plexus – Personal Identity / Ego & Mental Body

4. Heart Chakra – Social Identity / Community, Sharing & Connection

5. Throat Chakra – Spiritual Self Identity / Seeking Higher Truth & Greater Expression

6. Third Eye – Expanded Universal Identity / Seeing, Expanded Vision

7. Crown Chakra – Connection to Divine Identity / Knowing & Receiving Higher Truths

CHAPTER II

SUMMATION
OF WORKS

Y ou advance spiritually through the first seven levels of consciousness, your seven chakra bodies held within the lower
self, at a pace and manner that matches the level of your
intentions and effort. The quality of your intentions and amount of
effort you put into your spiritual evolvement determines the speed
and outcome of your results. Working through the seven chakra bodies
is about developing and preparing your spirit to exist and become
present within your physical life. By learning from your physical
existence, you learn acceptance within the various dimensions that
allows you to resonate your true self.

Once you have attained the basic foundations of arithmetic, you
incorporate them into the learning of algebra, geometry, trigonometry,
until you reach advanced stages of calculus and more complex studies of
mathematics and physics. You don't remain pondering the revelation of
$1+1=2$, but you build on your foundation of understanding to continue

to learn. This is similar to the way your spirit builds the foundation of your consciousness through each experience. What you do, how you perceive, and what you believe (your attachments) dictate the speed and outcome in the development of your consciousness. Your consciousness advances through the process of transitioning older paradigms to accept new ones as you evolve spiritually. You must leave behind what is comfortable and allow yourself to grow through the wisdom of your experiences on the way to obtaining higher consciousness. Since most of this growth is based on learning by acquiring experience, it becomes the premise of works. It is hard to ascend levels of consciousness without mentally processing and incorporating them into your life as you recreate your reality at each new level of existence.

It is not simply a matter of reconnecting back to your spiritual truths. Just because you understand something does not mean you consciously follow your understanding or your truths consistently and thoroughly. The initial transition from one form to another, spirit to physical, is a tremendous feat in itself. It would be similar to being relocated to a new country that has a different language, culture and way of life, with very little to no preparation. You would have to assimilate new ways of communicating, adapting and acclimating to the cultural, social, and political rules of your new environment. Similarly, there are many steps for you to take as you develop through the experiences of your life and the development of your emotional body and mental body to reach the energetic feeling body within your spirit. These are the building blocks that allow you to assimilate the energetic information of your environment. Until you have gained a better understanding and control of the physical, emotional and mental bodies in relation to your environment, you remain a prisoner to the undeveloped and separated fragments of your lower levels of consciousness that falsely direct and empower your ego.

Learning about concepts is only one part of actual understanding, similar to learning about a subject in school. In applying learning to a real life scenario, the process and outcome can be easy or difficult, depending on your perspective as your experiences unfold. It can be especially difficult the first time around. Each time you are exposed to the same conditioning, the experience becomes easier and easier until it is mastered. Each building block that you master allows for new blocks to be added to the knowledge, growth and development of your life and your spirit.

Some things that you experience in life are effortless, while other lessons keep repeating over and over again to a point of frustration. When you attach to the frustration of your experiences and your self-created illusions, you are experiencing the debt of your karmic lessons. Everything you see, act, and attach to adversely in your life is a product of your karma. You attract negative or positive attachment to the illusions in your lessons until what you are experiencing becomes clear within you. Once you achieve clarity, then you can choose to let go of the lesson. Experiencing karma can be as easy or as difficult as you choose to make it. The more lessons that you create for yourself by attaching to your life experiences, the more work you create for yourself, which can delay your spiritual growth and development. Remember, you create every experience that you encounter through your mental-emotional attachments to your experiences. This is what creates your illusion, because you have the freedom to attach to your experience with any emotion that you choose. From the first moment you open your eyes to the moment you take your last breath, you are given the choice of experiencing illusion or choosing awareness with each new experience. We often choose to act within our self-created illusions, and we empower them with our emotions, judgments and perceptions—worlds within worlds, our very own experiences of heaven and hell.

With each choice you make, you expose yourself to different degrees of energies within the experience of your illusions; this binds you to the law of attraction. If energy is neither created nor destroyed, then it is attracted, morphed and transferred into different forms. If you do *this*, you get *that*. Action creates reaction in a perpetual cycle that empowers the ego to motivate you in whichever direction you choose. If over stimulated, the ego can project a false mental-emotional perception of dominance over you. This false reality of ego exists until you are able to recognize, redirect and balance the energies of your spiritual fragments within yourself.

When you base your life in the realm of works, whether physical or spiritual, then your life is dependent on your perceived outcome. All of your experiences are illusions, empowered by your mental-emotional attachments. Your attachments create your lessons within your current level of consciousness. These are experiences that hold a lesson for you to learn and spiritually evolve. So, even if you attach, life will bring you more experiences to continue to give you the chance to learn and grow beyond your attachment. The perceived reality of your life is self-created and self-empowered by the consciousness level of your ego. You have the ability to choose to raise your consciousness, and choose which energies and lessons you want to support and learn from. You have the choice to learn how to flow through life effortlessly or remain mentally bound to the results of your experience. Every minute you use to emotionally empower and attach to your perceived negative experiences is time and energy taken from empowering positive growth in your life. When you pause to identify and wallow over perceived failure, loss, or disappointment, you are making a judgment on yourself that says, "I am not enough."

If someone steals from you, you may feel a sense of violation or injustice. If someone lies to you, you may feel a sense of betrayal. If someone physically or mentally abuses you, you may feel a sense of anger, weakness, or resentment. In essence, you empower a sense of fear that binds you prisoner to your experiences. Being a prisoner or victim to your life circumstances takes away the power and trust in you. By empowering the truths of others, you limit your ability to capably empower your spirit and your truths.

Where you place yourself in acceptance of your current consciousness is a direct result of your perceptions, beliefs, and illusions. You feed the realities and illusions of your life in order to learn from them. You can separate yourself from your illusions by using the awareness of your spiritual presence to redirect the ego. In the lower levels of your chakra system (chakras 1-4), your spirit is still adapting to your physical life. It is still developing your thoughts, intelligence, and emotional processes, so that you can later develop wisdom within your choices and discernment. Like a child that is still learning about life, responsibility, and accountability, your spirit has yet to fully integrate its spiritual wisdom into your physical existence. As you grow and develop your thoughts and emotions, you develop the responsibility and accountability of your spiritual wisdom. You are temporarily spiritually separated from everything around you, because your conscious awareness is still separated within your spirit.

Do you view yourself as separate and individual from your spirit and from others around you? Survival consciousness within you claims self-preservation as you empower your underdeveloped ego. As you begin to discover your identity within the physical existence, you realize that the life that you know is simply an expression of your accepted reality. This theory becomes true in the sense that you empower your own illusions, based upon the way you empower the ego, because you perceive your mental reality as real. If you did not exist within the physical body, which allows you to sense and feel, then the perception of your physical reality would not exist either. When you are able to detach from the control of your mental reality, then you free yourself from the limitations of physical existence. You begin to advance your spiritual existence and become unified to your higher consciousness as you increase your vibration and your spiritual presence. As you interact within your developing vibration, you allow yourself to experience the foundational learning blocks of your genetic spiritual evolution.

The spiritual resonation of your consciousness allows you to interact within the energetic field your environment creates for attraction and direction in your life. As you develop your spiritual vibration, you attract the necessary lessons and experiences at each level of consciousness development that help you to continue your evolution. You vibrationally affect the energetic field around you, as well as its consciousness resonation. When you raise your vibration, you affect the energetic field of your environment and help raise the consciousness vibration of your community. You become part of the whole and not separate to the self within your consciousness. Notice the positive and negative flows of conscious energy levels all around you. When you enter a sporting event, a music concert, a social or political venue, the general degree of emotion, interest, and conscious involvement that you experience is based upon like-mind, like-consciousness resonation that directs and sways the mood of the group or audience. You affect your environment or it affects you, depending on which vibration is higher.

You are the only factor that impedes your advancement through the levels of your consciousness. Through what you are taught, what you learn, and what you experience, you gather vibrations of consciousness that can create growth or limitations within your own consciousness. You can raise or lower your spiritual vibration at will. Since you are the creator of your physical and mental realities, you dictate the pace of your advancement by your attachment to reality and your perceptions. What you accept as truths becomes your reality. Your truths can limit or free the pure potential of your divinity and that of enlightenment. Because humanity has chosen to progress through a system of perceived works, we feel that we need to measure, sense and process the experiences of our development. We mentally believe advancement must be achieved, instead of choosing the simplicity of acknowledging the power of who we are, and then accepting this knowledge as a part of us.

If you wait for your mind to process each experience that you encounter, you delay your own potential of unfolding. Mental processing of every experience means waiting many lifetimes in order to experience your divinity through reincarnation. Just as you know the sun rises and the sun sets, you are able to see it rise and experience its warmth without having to know everything about how it works. Although you may have a sense of the effects of the sun within this physical world, you are likely not aware of all that it does for you within your body, for the Earth and the universe. Just like any physical object or being in the universe, the sun plays a direct role not only in its own existence, but in balancing all existence in some form or another simply by being present. You do not need to understand all the workings of the sun in order to reap its benefits, its warmth, its properties for life and growth, or its importance of magnetic symmetry for the solar system's existence. Similarly, you do not need to mentally process all of your experiences but rather just accept them and move on to the next experience. This allows you further growth and brings you closer to knowing your true self. The ability to choose to live your life or allow life to choose for you is in the daily choices that you make to increase or delay your growth and development, your spiritual evolvement. It is a matter of choice that holds you responsible for the development and direction of your life.

The presence of who you are is dictated by the level of your vibration, because you live and act within the level of consciousness that you attach to. It is not a matter of what you do, whether you are kind or cruel, but who you are that helps or hinders you as an individual and a part of society. The vibration you give off interacts with the general summation of vibrations around you and adjusts to it accordingly. A woman who expresses a fit of rage can affect the people around her. Everyone reacts and alters his or her persona to accommodate that elevated state of emotional vibration. If this same woman loses her job, she may lower her own vibration by feeling angry, depressed, or expressing self-pity. The emotions of her lower conscious state can affect the consciousness of her environmental support. If she is feeling angry and reacts by yelling and screaming at her family, she is expressing the effects of her lowered vibration that has affected her self-worth. Something that isn't picked up right away or food that is being wasted causes unnecessary fits of rage, because she may feel unworthy and revert back to survival. Her reality becomes a direct reflection of her vibration, of her inner self-worth, and a reflection of her current state of spiritual consciousness. Her spiritual energies are no longer in balance. The spiritual fragments scream inside from self-inflicted mental poverty. This unbalanced energy manifests itself outwardly so that others can hear the affects of her internal suffering and pain. Is there a direct correlation between these multiple actions and the events that led up to the loss of this person's job? Perhaps. We humans tend to mirror our inward intent toward our outward behavioral manifestation. People who react negatively can force their vibrations upon others without even knowing it, simply by attaching to their experience negatively and then wallowing in that negativity. This becomes the driving motivational force of the ego, based on self-preservation—a falsely empowered ego.

Your vibrational expressions and intentions are seen in snippets in the ways you think and act, and in what you surround yourself with. When you live within a world of self-preservation, you draw forth lower levels of consciousness to manifest within your life. The force that drives and builds a company, a city or a nation is derived from the collective vibrations of the people who manifest its creation. A system built on self-preservation, greed and the need to control must constantly stroke its own ego as well as the egos of its supporters, workers and the general public. It must continually fuel the machine with rewards that promote greed. A company that is built on integrity, goodwill and acceptance of its pure potentiality guides and masters its direction in the knowing and worth of its products or services. It adds to society simply because positive intentions add to the vibration rather than take away or feed off of other people.

The mere intention of your thoughts and actions changes your vibration, based out of your emotional motive. When you act out of love and abundance, you live in acceptance, happiness and peace. You may treat someone to lunch or dinner simply out of a desire to give. This act of kindness then adds to the two energies and increases the vibration and trust that benefits both people, the giver and the receiver. The same act of offering lunch or dinner with the intention of an expected return lowers the vibration of the union and, therefore, requires constant energy to maintain the relationship. Continual stroking of the other party's ego is required. If you each work out of different intents on the same act, a miscommunication occurs depending upon who is giving and who is receiving. Nothing is added or taken away, and no direction is created for the flowering of growth. Both parties drain each other, because you are working out of different vibrations of intention. So in order for forward motion to occur within any level of vibration, you attract those of like-mind and repel those of unlike-mind. You can only exist at your level of consciousness when you attract others at the same level or lower, until you are ready for growth.

As you advance levels of consciousness, a period of disarray may take place as the body transitions itself to hold higher vibrations. The things that have worked in the past may no longer provide the same results as higher frequencies are added to the body. Your worlds come crashing down on you momentarily as you learn to hold higher frequencies. Some panic and try to revert back to what is comfortable or known, but as you incorporate higher frequencies, you are held at a higher accountability. One cannot go back to learning arithmetic when trying to master algebra. Although arithmetic is a building block for learning algebra, it is a learned trait from your past and becomes remedial in your growth. It is a learned trait that is needed, but has become something that you have no need to re-experience.

As you raise your level of consciousness, you take on new knowledge, paradigms and realities. They hold you more accountable to yourself. As you advance through the first seven levels of consciousness, you activate and take on various parts of yourself, parts that you have always had within you. If you encounter delay in the process of your evolvement, it is because of the many boundaries and limitations that you place in your mind through your thoughts, judgments, and attachments. What you input into your mind and body through your thoughts and perceptions adapts to the vibrational frequencies that you resonate. The things that you think, act, and surround yourself with help to regulate or hinder the frequency that you vibrate. The power of your thoughts cannot be underestimated. You must learn to empower your thoughts to remove your boundaries of mental limitations and attachments.

We're often told that in order to succeed in a profession or skill, we must surround ourselves with the right people as well as learn from those who have succeeded and mastered the same things we pursue. This is why people pay millions of dollars every year to learn from professionals in their area of interest. The pressure starts when we've made a commitment to improve ourselves both physically and mentally for anything that we may desire, and the same goes for developing your spiritual vibrations. You make a commitment to yourself and find solutions for whatever is needed to come forth to help assist in allowing for this change.

Sometimes you may feel empowered by the knowledge of this vibration. Other times you dread it, because it forces you to look at yourself. You may not like what you see. Knowing that change is necessary makes you vulnerable and transparent not only to yourself, but to the people around you. When you take on new levels of consciousness, you leave behind the things that are familiar and become vulnerable to your surroundings and the people that you've known. As your consciousness changes, you are no longer able to recognize or relate to certain people familiar to you, because you are no longer resonating at their level of comfort or familiarity.

Taking on and assimilating any level of consciousness, whether higher or lower, alters your present level of perception. What is true at one level can be completely different within the understanding of another level, depending upon your acquired perception or surroundings. You cannot go to a foreign county and expect to immediately understand the differences in culture. What is normal for them might not be something supported by your social experience and programming. This also applies to the adaptation of levels of consciousness. You take on various parts of yourself on a spiritual level and express its characteristics outwardly in your present life. Your intelligence expands along with your expression and is directed in whichever way your spirit allows it to unfold. It takes time to adapt to changes in your consciousness. The further you advance your paths or vibrations, the more unique and specific you become. You gain more insight and understanding to your origin and realize who you are, and can begin unlocking yourself from within.

If you entered your physical existence with psychic gifts, you may have been immediately confronted by roadblocks from the social surroundings you adapted into. Depending on how you were nurtured through your adolescence, you either evolved with your personal gifts intact or shifted to lower levels of consciousness. The core within you never changes, only the adaptation of who you are within your surroundings affects and dictates your growth to higher levels of vibration. Because you live in a world with so many diverse people of varying cultures, backgrounds, and levels of consciousness, there is no continuity in the development of your own spirituality. You first and foremost struggle with understanding your own ego and the role it plays within your growth of understanding who you are. Then you are subjected to the millions of undeveloped egos within people that you encounter and interact with on a regular basis, people who base their egos within the foundations of their own experiences and the teachings that they may adhere to within the textbooks of man-made religions and philosophies. This complex dynamic plays a role in the balance and development of the Earth's population in spiritual growth and the evolution of society.

Within this lifetime, you can choose to break past the web of societal control set in this world and reconnect back to who you were to begin with: your higher self or, in essence, your own divinity. At the sixth level of consciousness, the third eye, you begin to expose yourself to higher vibrations past the five senses of the human body. The realms past the physical world lie within the astral realm or the non-physical and multi-dimensional universe. These realms are full of spirits, guides, demons, angels and much more. There are also struggles within this hierarchy of existence. No thought should be given to the idea that the inhabitants of these realms are smarter or more aware than you are in the physical realm. They are simply not bound within physical bodies. Just as you attract and empower the people around you, you also empower these beings in order for them to exist or affect your life. If you empower their energy or vibration, you give recognition to their existence, and then you give away your own power and identity. There are also many non-physical spiritual guides and masters to assist you along your path. However, these true teachers only point the way and never drain you of your energies.

Light and dark exist in balance and are only swayed when you empower energies in either direction. There is no predetermined direction, only the direction in which you empower. If you choose through your perceptions and beliefs to become a conduit or vehicle for other energies within your consciousness resonation, then you can allow them to take control of your mind and body. They will take advantage of your thoughts and actions in order to manifest what they want to express. Your true power resides within you and *only* you. The higher self is the highest expression of who you are and your purpose here on Earth. You and *only* you can make every decision involving your life, and when you sync up to your higher vibration, your purpose and your life evolves. If you believe your life to be overseen or judged by a higher force outside of you, then you become a victim to circumstance and the negative energies that would love to invade your physical world.

When you take on the accountability and responsibility of your highest expression past the sixth level of consciousness, you enter your crown and receive from your higher self. Here resides the doorway to enlightenment and higher levels of consciousness beyond the lower physical self. Past the works of the seven levels of consciousness and the doorway to enlightenment are the levels of awareness. These are no longer based upon works, but upon knowing who you are and whether you are worthy and humble enough in accepting your highest vibrations. This is when the unification of the spirit occurs, such as in the trials and tribulations of Master Jesus in the desert and Master Buddha under the Bodhi tree. As you progress further within your spiritual evolution, knowing the self becomes a test of your ability to experience, receive, accept, and be accountable for the balance of energies in the world around you. Within the levels of enlightenment beyond the seventh level of consciousness into the levels of the higher self, you are tested for any limitations of acceptance within you, in order for your spirit to be fully present within your physical existence. As you continue along the journey, you are tested to verify your unconditional acceptance of your entire self.

CHAPTER 12

CONTINUING THE JOURNEY

The first seven levels of consciousness make up what is called the lower self or physical self. They are constructed from the spiritual makeup of your seven lower chakra bodies which create your spirit's roadmap within the human experience. Together, the chakras are a learning medium for you to experience the integration of your spiritual and physical existence from a level of works. Experiencing your life allows you to learn and understand all of the different parts of yourself, the various dimensions within you that allow for your spirit to further add to and expand its knowledge and wisdom. In ascending the first seven levels of consciousness, you begin the initial ground work of integrating your spiritual self to your physical self. As you experience and unite your lower spiritual fragments (your chakra bodies), you learn and understand how to master yourself.

Before you separated from universal consciousness to experience the essence of creation, you were unified spirit. You were an expression of infinite balance and completion, masculine and feminine, light and dark, yin and yang. Your human life allows you to experience all the wonder and knowledge that creation has to offer as it unfolds. As you entered your physical body, your spirit splits or fragments itself into the various expressions of the chakra bodies, just as your spirit splits its physical expression into being either male or female. In the birthing of your physical self, you do not lose your full spiritual expression, but infuse it within your energetic makeup that supports the balance of the spiritual body within the physical body. Because you are already spiritually complete within your entire energetic makeup, you have the same ability to achieve levels of consciousness that ascended masters of the past accomplished in their lifetimes. In raising the vibration of your consciousness, you allow yourself to receive the presence of your divine spirit. This shows you who you truly are. The ability to resonate at the level of your divine presence grants you access to the wisdom of your higher self. Your higher self is your spiritual wisdom that is interwoven within the fabric of universal consciousness.

When you entered your physical existence, you began the journey of experiencing creation through your spiritual unfolding. Learning from the starting point of creation allows you to grow and develop at your desired rate of learning, managing and taking on the responsibility of your spiritual potential. When you are birthed into creation, both spiritually and physically, you begin to mold yourself. Everything in the universe and life is there to help support this process. As you advance through learning and experiencing life, your spirit evolves with you as you grow and develop through the experience. You begin your experience at the level of survival as you build information within each experience to move forward in life. Foundational lessons of survival must be learned and experienced in order to develop responsibility in you. Some children are born wise and take on their responsibilities with ease, while others struggle into adulthood with the inability to survive and be responsible. The difference seen in your spirit's ability of acceptance, lifetime to lifetime, creates your karmic experiences within your levels of consciousness. From your stages of infancy, childhood into adulthood, you build your wisdom through the lessons of your experiences. When you have shown a level of knowledge and responsibility that matches your current level of consciousness, you advance to the next stage of consciousness development.

Not everyone advances their consciousness equally with the passing of time. In fact, there are many people who choose to stay within the comfort and responsibility of their lower realms of consciousness. Each level of consciousness holds you to a different level of responsibility for your life. The responsibility at each level of consciousness is similar to comparing the responsibility that an employee has versus a manager or owner of a company. Each level of function holds a different degree of responsibility. You choose to evolve your level of consciousness with each new experience you encounter. You choose the level of your responsibility within the programs of your current level of consciousness. At lower levels of consciousness, you may choose to be a victim, behave as a child, and throw tantrums or fits based on your accepted level of responsibility within yourself. Your lower level of consciousness development causes you to react this way when you don't get what you want, or when things don't go your way. It can cause you to make up excuses or tell lies when you are not able to follow through with commitments or responsibilities. You choose to blame others for the circumstances of your life, your failures and your faults. Do you know people who act or behave like this? Do you sometimes behave this way? When you are spiritually regressing, it is easy to point the finger of responsibility and blame the world for all your problems. Your negative perception of yourself causes you to attract negativity into your life and remove accountability for yourself and the circumstances of your life. To fully understand the consciousness development of your spirit within your physical life, you have to accept a more complete view of your spiritual evolvement. You must view your physical existence at the level of spiritual awareness.

In fully understanding your spiritual growth, you need to understand it in every aspect of your life and why you have chosen to come here and evolve. Now that you have been introduced to the seven chakras, you are ready to learn about other aspects of your spiritual makeup to develop a more holistic view of the lower self. The seven levels of consciousness development explained through the lower chakra system is only one aspect of your spiritual makeup.

Beyond the chakras, you must understand the need for balance and the need for opposites, masculine and feminine, light and dark, the spirit's energy body at the levels of attraction and expression. You must understand the spiritual development of your "ego," the part of you that drives your need to survive and succeed in the physical existence at every level of consciousness. You must also understand the relationship between the physical self and spiritual self at each level of existence within the lower self. Without a complete understanding of what you are spiritually, your puzzle of spiritual evolvement will have missing pieces of information. These gaps of information can cause confusion and misunderstanding, leading you down a path of failure or a dead end. Like skipping a chapter or two in a book, you may not fully comprehend or understand its meaning or concept. Without full knowledge and acceptance within yourself, you cannot be free from the attachment of your false identity—the human existence. You cannot achieve complete awareness in the presence of your spirit, and the levels of enlightenment within yourself.

The second half of this book will explain the missing links of your spiritual evolvement, the information that will lead you away from roadblocks and dead ends along your path of spiritual evolution. Anything rejected or seen as separate from you stalls spiritual growth. Until you are able to learn to accept yourself completely, you cannot find the presence of God within your spirit—the presence of your divinity.

CHAPTER 13

TWO-WAY MIRROR

O nce you reach the crown chakra, you reach the doorway to enlightenment, but have not entered. The question then becomes, how far up the spiritual ladder do you really want to go? To reach the consciousness level of the crown chakra is a difficult task within itself, yet it is the intermediate step towards achieving enlightenment. Most people who have reached this level of awareness are happy to receive from a higher source of existence and communicate with their spiritual guides. However, to be able to unite your higher self and descend it into the physical self is to experience greater levels of enlightenment within you. With this level of wisdom and understanding, you are able to be present and obtain multiple dimensions of awareness in your life. In choosing to advance further, you step out of your karmic life lessons held within your chakra bodies and begin the journey through the higher levels of your spiritual consciousness. To be free of your karma is to be free of your mental-emotional attachments and life lessons. In entering the mirror of your spiritual consciousness, you learn to become living spirit. Within these higher levels of consciousness, you become the creator of the self. Every thought, action and notion becomes the reality of your awareness. This is a huge responsibility to take on because it means being fully responsible and accountable for yourself.

At higher levels of consciousness, you are detached from the results of your experiences and its outcomes. You become fully present. Your spirit allows for synchronicity to take place and manifests people and events into your life at their appropriate time. You become free from forcing or stalling yourself within the prison of your mental-emotional mind. As you ascend the levels towards your divinity, you increase your vibrations, thereby allowing more of your spiritual gifts to manifest within the body. The higher you are able to vibrate, the more magical your gifts become until you reach the levels of infinite possibilities within the physical body.

Very few people in the world have achieved the higher levels of vibration beyond the development of the seven chakras or have been able to master their spiritual vibrations to add to the vibrational makeup of humankind. In fact, only a fraction of the world's population has achieved such levels of higher consciousness. These masters coexist among us to help maintain energetic balance for the planet as they raise vibrational consciousness within themselves. They do not seek recognition or praise. At this level of consciousness, the ego becomes wisdom and completes the triune of your divinity. The three layers of the spirit are balanced.

In biblical terms, the triune exists as the Father, Son, and the Holy Spirit. In metaphysics, the triune consists of the middle self, inner child, and higher self. In today's language, it is referenced as the conscious, subconscious, and higher conscious. The subconscious inner child holds all the information from your past lives, past experiences and development of your emotional body and its developing ego. The conscious middle self assimilates the energetic information from your current experiences. It is the part of you that uses the information stored within your mental body that adds to the knowledge and strength of your experiencing ego as you learn to parent your life. The higher conscious of your higher self is the wisdom that guides your life in its spiritual evolution. Hence, there are many ways to describe the makeup of the spirit, such as from the aspects of the chakras or the three layers of spirit. Regardless of whether you describe the human body from its outer appearance, inner physiology, or cellular makeup, they are all correct descriptive aspects of describing the structure of the human body. None is more correct than the other, but merely a perspective from which to describe the body and the many layers of its function and expression. Similarly, understanding different perspectives of the spirit's construct provides for greater comprehension and awareness.

When your physical self is guided by your divine presence and driven by a fully developed and balanced ego, you walk the Earth as the masters who had traveled before you. You add to and harmonize the vibrations and energies around you. Raising the levels of your vibrations allows for the flowering of consciousness. Higher vibrations then enter the world and affect the total level of consciousness for the evolvement of humanity. You have seen this in people such as Mother Theresa, Mahatma Gandhi, the Dalai Lama and many others who have made a significant impact in changing the world for the better. They were spiritually present. How many lives have they changed and motivated simply by living their higher purpose? We all have a tendency to seek purpose within our lives as well as the reason for our lives. The biggest question always asked is, "What is my purpose here in the world?" In essence, the only purpose for any of us to achieve is to discover and express who we are. Every second that your life unfolds brings you one step closer to learning more about yourself. Within that discovery, you find how you may serve humanity for its highest purpose.

When you take the first steps beyond the consciousness levels of your lower seven chakras, you open up a doorway into learning and experiencing balance. You experience the individual characteristics of your spiritual development working in unison at its highest function. The union and equality within the different energies of your spiritual fragments work in harmony for you and empower you. Similar to running a business, there are different levels of roles and responsibilities that need to be in place to make a successful business run efficiently. If your spiritual fragments remained separated, it causes resistance or stalled growth. If each chakra body that holds specific functional processes and responsibilities is performing optimally, their combined energies direct the momentum of your spirit and your life for further growth. When living within the separation and self identity of an individual spiritual fragment, you cause internal conflict within yourself. Your spiritual separation, the separation of your energies, causes confusion and lack of direction within the self. You begin to work against yourself, which causes you to view the world around you as a struggle. In the same sense, energetic imbalance represents an internal conflict within you.

When you have resistance against someone or something, you must ask yourself, "Why do I feel this emotional resistance?" Within this question, you should be able to come up with a number of excuses or blame that seems to justify the reason for resistance. Then you should follow this with the question, "How long am I going to hold on to and empower this negativity?" These emotional anchors are the energies that do not allow you to be completely free to view your life and everything within it as a means of support. The optimal perspective is the ability to see each learning experience as the chance for you to strengthen and grow.

The doorway to enlightenment, the final steps toward becoming fully enlightened is not an easy journey, nor an entirely blissful one. Master Buddha achieved levels of higher consciousness within his spirit under the Bodhi tree. He faced all of his demons, represented by Mara, and overcame all the separated dimensions within himself. Master Buddha experienced and accepted the infinite dimensions of his spirit. He overcame the temptation of identity that exists within lower levels of consciousness thinking, labeling and judging that exist within spiritual separation.

As you achieve the levels of higher consciousness within your spirit, you gain levels of enlightenment as you experience the many dimensions of your spirit that allow for harmony and balance within the self. At each level of higher consciousness you are spiritually tested to see what degree of union and acceptance you have within yourself. Each chakra body within the lower self represents the different developmental stages of your physical and spiritual progression. The ladder of your spiritual progression allows you to descend the wisdom of your higher self into your physical presence. This is made up of tests that reflect the level of your current knowledge and understanding of acceptance at each level of consciousness. It tests the degree of acceptance and resistance within yourself as you descend your higher self. In removing all resistance within yourself, you expand the boundaries of your consciousness into unconditional awareness and acceptance of existence. You become conscious and aware that all things have purpose. You come to know that the labels or judgments of good and bad, light and dark, are necessary for learning and experiencing what life has to offer for your balance, understanding and growth. These dualities create the balance of opposites that bring forth creation and life. As only male and female expressions can create union in order to give life, you begin to learn the balance and union of creation within yourself.

When you take the first steps in the union of your masculine and feminine parts, the balance of energy within yourself, you essentially start from the ground floor and work your way back up to the top. This is nothing that you have to do or become, but it is proof of who you are, and where your true nature lies. By being free of attachment and not empowering the lower vibrations that hold you to lower levels of resistance, you resonate forth your highest vibration. This assists in your tests at higher levels of consciousness. As Master Jesus confronted

Satan in the desert, he entered into the levels of higher consciousness within his own spirit that tested the wills of his spiritual fragments. You face yourself as you face the separate identities that exist within your spiritual fragments.

You are capable of everything and anything that you can imagine, whether you have experienced it or not within this lifetime. Within your physical experience, you face the worst and best of what you are capable of as you face the tests of your spirit. The many faces of your false identities within you challenge whether you are able to detach from the creation of your false illusions. The false identities of separation within you create the views of judgment and separation around you. In your exposure to pain and suffering, you learn degrees of acceptance. Whether suffering is directed towards you or at someone who is closest to you, you realize that all things have their own path of consciousness development that teaches balance. As you face the imbalance of your spiritual fragments and are able to let go, you remain unaffected by not allowing yourself to be swayed by your emotions or mental attachments. You may temporarily lose your psychic abilities during your tests, causing you to second-guess yourself. This tests the amount of trust you have in yourself and your ability to discern your truth from what is false within you. You trust in yourself and your own abilities to stand within your spirit's strength. You bring balance to your ego to remain strong in the presence and knowing of who you are.

When you combine the spirit of your wisdom and strength, you receive your masculine and feminine energies, which make up the true essence of the spirit's dual energies that displays balance in your presence. Together, they provide you with humility, compassion and strength for your purpose here in this world. As you become enlightened, you continually expand and express your infinite potential. You are not swayed by other people's perceptions and judgments of what you are. You can remain in acceptance and non-judgment, which further enhances the purpose for your presence amongst humankind. Directed by your divinity, you remain at peace and in harmony within yourself to serve all of humankind for the betterment of the whole versus the self. We are all here to learn and experience from one another as a family and not as separate individuals. When you gain levels of higher understanding and awareness, you see the cohesive connections that all have to offer. When you see yourself as whole, you offer others a little more compassion, a little more patience, and a little more acceptance within the family of spirit, the balance within the family that is God.

As you advance each step through the levels of your higher consciousness, you unite each level of higher conscious with your lower conscious in order to create balance within yourself. You come to understand the balance of light and dark, good and bad, the opposites of balance at all levels of consciousness. You see that one cannot exist without the other. If you never have known tremendous pain or suffering, you cannot understand compassion. You would not know the value of complete joy without the trials of suffering. The separation of judgment is labeled only within the interpretations of your mental attachments, within your limited thoughts and beliefs. Thought is understood and interpreted on many levels depending on the person viewing the experience. Even within the greatest perceived suffering, there is benefit on all levels. The only reason you hold onto the attachment of suffering is that your developing ego benefits from the constant emotional stimulation of your mentally inflicted suffering. Otherwise, you would have let it go the instant that you received it. Like a child, the young ego says, "Oh, woe is me. See how they have wronged me? See how unrighteous they are for doing this to me? See my pain and suffering? How can I be noticed because I need more attention?" Yet, the moment you let go of suffering, you release all the energy trapped within the negative vibration of suffering and move toward balance, towards positive growth and joy. They say time heals all wounds. In truth, until you heal your emotional wounds, time is used for the pride of your ego that holds onto suffering for the perceived benefit of the self.

When you realize that you attach and hold onto unnecessary pain and suffering, you realize that you have a choice. You can choose to step out of the emotional prison of your illusions. You can choose to free yourself, to move forward in life and learn acceptance from the lessons of your experience. Acceptance without judgment is the key to maintaining energy flow in your life. When you emotionally pause in life, you expose yourself to the possibility of becoming energetically stuck in the confusion of emotional turbulence. Without the waves of emotional turbulence that causes resistance, you allow balance, acceptance and growth into your life. When you are able to detach from other people's negative energies, you empower yourself and those around you. You are your greatest teacher, because you can determine how you interpret or act within the illusion of your life. Alcoholics gain no benefit from someone approving of their lifestyle, because they consciously choose to create internal and external destruction in their lives and the lives that they attach themselves to. Once they acknowledge that they have a problem and want to change, they can consciously decide to take the appropriate step to leave their self-created reality. You cannot force them to change. Change can only happen when a person observes and realizes that they are harming themselves and possibly the lives of others.

The relationships you create or take on mirror how you value yourself. The people that you admire or look up to have the same negative abilities as they do positive, because we are all equal in capability. The people that you dislike can represent the traits that you dislike or do not accept about yourself. It is through the lens of your own perception that you focus on the things you dislike in others. Therefore, acceptance of the people that you dislike can become your greatest reward in learning about yourself. Equally, when you reject your worst qualities, you empower them into existence in your life. The energetic thoughts and stimulation of that emotional energy draws it into manifestation in your life. It is the part of you that steps forward and shows itself in the animalistic nature of survival, pride or righteousness. Seen in the light of life as your teaching ground, this is all actually very good. Use your external experience to learn about yourself. Observe without judgment and try to understand the mystery that presents itself in your physical world so that you can learn about your own weaknesses and strengths. In this manner, you evolve quickly and move through life onto more adventures and growth.

In essence, you are here to learn all sides of yourself at various levels of your existence. Every thought or decision you make sends forth an energy or vibration to attract the lessons or outcomes for you to learn from and grow. By accepting the outcomes that your actions and decisions place you in, you speed up the lessons of acceptance within the various levels of your consciousness. One truth remains constant at every level of consciousness—you are only in control of *your* life and not the lives of the people you surround yourself with, nor the situations or events around you. When you experience resistance through force or stress, you experience it within your body. Whether this energy is being empowered by someone or something within your conscious perception, it increases energetic emotional stress within you. Whether expressed through anger, anxiety, pain or suffering, it is the vacillation of your energy as it moves towards imbalance. This imbalance is the empowerment of your various spiritual fragments, the chakra bodies that direct the way you react to the experience within your present level of consciousness. By empowering each fragment of the spirit individually, you cause a spiritual war within the self as a result.

We all enjoy the comforts of being recognized for who we are, whether it is with a simple thank you, a better job, or celebrity status. Similarly, each fragment of your spirit desires to be recognized and accepted within the physical self. However, your lower fragments desire more recognition than your non-judgmental higher parts that allow for existence to take place. Your life is a representation of your spiritual fragments and therefore, you are a vibrational representation of your karma. Within each of your fragments, there are lessons and purpose for its existence. When you unite all of your fragments as whole, you become whole and attract that which you are into your life. This helps you to direct your purpose. Seen in terms of a perfect circle, a circle holds substance within its boundaries, like a ball that holds air. If you remove a piece of the circle, you allow for the air to be released into the environment, causing the circle to loose shape and function. If the circle is maintained and complete, it can take on various functions. The creation of the circle empowers its intelligence to become anything and everything imaginable. It has morphed into wheels for mechanical use and transportation, balls for recreation, art sculptures for beauty. From small objects to big ones, everything is contained within the circle of life and creation, the union of your spiritual fragments.

When you conceive a child, you become accountable for this fragment of you. You care for your child, until he can depend on himself. You nurture, teach and provide for your child, because he is part of you. You learn to love and accept him as you both grow older and begin leading separate lives. And even if you sometimes disagree, you allow more room for acceptance and forgiveness, because he is a part of you. In the same sense, you must allow for more acceptance and forgiveness within yourself, because your spiritual fragments are an accumulation of who you are. To understand and accept the self is to understand that you are connected to and part of everyone and everything here, living and non-living.

Whatever you accomplish or allow for yourself offers up a frequency for the rest of us to learn and manifest from. What keeps us from total commonality is our own individual expressions. Not everyone in this world is meant for the same task, yet everyone in this world is capable of the same acceptance. There is a purpose for each individual's life. Whether you are a teacher, carpenter, ambassador or parent, you serve a purpose. You add to the life of everyone that you encounter. You learn through your experience and your experience allows others to learn more about themselves. You accelerate the learning experience by how fast you are able to accept and move forward in your life's lessons, until there is nothing more to learn in the complete unconditional acceptance of what you are. This allows for acceptance of everything around you and the acceleration of your spiritual growth.

There is no set formula for everyone to follow. There are only footprints left behind by others who have achieved such levels. Understanding the paths of the past gives us clues about how to proceed in the present. It is easier to follow the footprints of others, utilizing the information they have left behind for those who are willing to follow. Although, a word of caution is warranted. Following others also leaves room for you to fail and remove your accountability within the path of self discovery. Just like the transfer of information from one person to another, the translation of teachings can become misconstrued and misinterpreted to sound right for the masses versus being truthful for the individual. A simple sentence can be misinterpreted, depending upon how a verbal inflection or tone is used or even how a word is perceived and understood by each individual. A thought or idea can be altered, depending upon the person's level of understanding of the subject. The meaning of a principle can be misunderstood when it is translated from one language to another. It is how the same truths that have been repeated by several messengers over the millennia have been segregated, misinterpreted, and divided. And now they are being used by one group of humans against another in the name of human pride, defined within human-interpretation of religion or philosophy.

So where does this leave you in the quest for awareness and enlightenment? The primary message in the majority of religious teachings and philosophies relays the concept of self-discovery, whether you want to call it "God," "Buddha," "Nirvana," "Dharma," or whatever else. In essence, these teachings describe the principles of the divine self.

Obtaining one's divinity can be summed up in a few sentences. To live a life of unconditional acceptance is to live a life that allows you to detach from self-created illusions that hinder your ability to exist in peace and happiness. Your roadmap to enlightenment found within yourself is not the same path traveled by the majority of spiritual seekers, because it is a roadmap especially designed by you, for you. There is no set roadmap to obtaining the divine self within you. Your vibrations increase as you obtain each new level of consciousness, allowing you to detach from your previous consciousness. Growth comes naturally as you evolve your consciousness. Growth is the expression of life and the spirit; it is a part of everything that surrounds you. The only true path is the path that is right for you and only you, for this is the path of discovering your true self.

In your own self-discovery, you find the truth to the existence of balance and life. You understand the reason for existence—opposites and equality. When you discover your own truths, you reconnect back to universal truths. You understand why you need to experience suffering just as much as you need to experience joy. The need to experience yourself begins with recognizing that where you are at this present time is where you are supposed to be. This is what makes you perfect for you on your given path. Self-discovery coincides with evolvement of the self. When you are ready to pick up the next piece of the puzzle, then you will know that it is the appropriate time. Until you reach the doorway to enlightenment, you get to enjoy the experience of all that life has to offer. Whether it is through the mystery of love with a partner, the joy of giving birth to a child or the pain of losing someone you love, you experience the self. We all have the ability to live continuously in the balance of maintaining harmony within the universe and within ourselves. To know thyself is to experience what "God" experiences: your divinity. Having divine presence is being able to experience unconditional love and acceptance in all that has been created in order for you to experience creation. In order to know this, you must understand the relationship of the spirit within the physical existence, the next layer of understanding the process on the road to enlightenment.

CHAPTER 14

THE SPIRITUAL-
PHYSICAL
RELATIONSHIP

When you understand the inception of the spirit and how it relates to the physical body, you know the self. As previously explored, you are made up of moving charged vibrational particles of matter that make up the resonance of the spirit for physical expression. You experience your environment as tangible, because everything that is physical around you resonates at similar vibrational frequencies. It is not until your spirit enters your physical body that it becomes bound in reference to experiencing physical matter. When you stub your toe against a wall, for instance, the two similar vibrations of your toe and the wall collide and disrupt each other's vibrational frequency. This elicits a physical expression of pain, swelling or bruising, which is caused by a shift in your physical frequency. Because your body and the wall exist in the same frequency range, that of physical expression, you collide with rather than pass through the wall.

Let's explore how else two different frequencies or energies affect one another. In physics, we know that the process of induction occurs when a positive or negative charged object is brought near a neutral object. The neutral object's electron structure becomes affected by the charged object. The presence of the charged object can affect the presence of the neutral object, forcing its electrons to react to the charge of the opposing object. This leaves an unbalanced charge within the neutral object unless a ground is brought near to release the affected charge.

Consider these two objects as two people, you and an angry person; you each have two different sets of emotionally charged resonations. When you come into close proximity with an angry person, depending upon how you are feeling, you and your body can react towards this angry person in many different ways. Your level of consciousness dictates your reaction to the expressions of the angry person; you may choose to assist, avoid or defensively react to the angry person. Your positive and negative consciousness perception, thoughts and intentions emit your physical body's reaction when coming into vibrational contact with another person's consciousness resonation. Your physical body is energetically affected by the vibrational frequencies of your surrounding energy field and the people within it. This is how your spiritual or energy body assimilates and affects the magnetic energy field around you.

When you entered your physical body by lowering your spirit's vibrational frequencies to resonate at the level of your physical body's frequencies, your body becomes the conductor that harnesses your projected spiritual body. Your physical body becomes a neutral conductor that houses your spiritual vibrations at all levels of consciousness. As you input your positive or negative thoughts or intentions, you send out frequencies that change the charge of your physical body through the transmission of your spiritual vibrational frequencies. Your vibrationally-charged body then communicates to your vibrational surroundings and affects it accordingly. Equally, just as you can affect your physical surroundings, so too can your physical surroundings have an effect on you. Depending on the level of vibrational frequency that you choose to resonate at, whether you vibrate higher or lower than your surroundings, you can attract or repel things based upon your vibrational frequencies. When you resonate at higher frequencies, you are able to null or void lower frequencies, because higher spiritual frequencies are faster moving particles that are less easily affected by lower physical frequencies. When you choose to raise or lower your frequencies based on the level of consciousness that you choose to evoke, you can raise and lower your affinity with various attractions that may manifest within your life.

When you enter an environment that you perceive as negative, your spirit prepares you vibrationally to become more focused and mentally aware of your surroundings. In this manner, your spirit helps you avoid negative attraction. At the same time, if you resonate at lower level frequencies, you cannot help but attract negative manifestation. A strong negative conductor or a person resonating at lower levels of consciousness will emit an excess of negative expressions that manifest or attract negative experiences and outcomes. This is not to say that such a person is bad so bad things happen to them. The person is simply acting out of a lower level of consciousness and therefore, attracts the negative lessons or experiences that are there to help him or her grow. The expression of negativity is represented in physical acts of dominance and survival consciousness that drain the overall energy field of an individual's surroundings.

Someone who resonates at higher levels of consciousness will emit positive vibrational frequencies that add to the energy field of their surroundings. The majority of the population exists in the middle of these two extremes, where equal exchanges of energies are needed to continually balance the self. We become dependent upon each other for gain and balance that provides for our needs. This becomes a means of survival within the world. The act of giving and exchanging is an act of balance and coexistence of the population's individual abilities to provide support and function within and between communities. The ability to work and do work in exchange for money or services, applying one's function to receive sustenance for survival, that is the current benefit of relationships within the human community.

Induction and energy exchange also occur at a cellular level. A living cell is simply a smaller manifestation of the physical body. The input that the physical body provides to the cell directs its expression as well as its function. When a physical manifestation forms in the womb through the union of two cells that exchange different vibrational frequencies, the resulting fetus becomes a conductor for positive or negative vibrational frequency exchange. Therefore, teaching and molding a child begins at the embryonic stage of development and is further enhanced during the rest of the pregnancy. There are many tools and books written about how to stimulate awareness within the unborn child. Through the sounds and vibrations of classical music such as the works of Mozart, as well as reading and speaking to the child within the womb, research has shown that these inputs can stimulate brain development within the unborn child. When a mother raises or lowers her vibrational frequency, she transfers this information to her unborn infant as well.

So, just as you can be affected by external vibrational frequencies in a positive or negative manner, a mother can also affect her infant's vibrational frequency in the same way. If she ingests excessive amounts of drugs or alcohol, she can create pre-dependencies, congenital defects or brain deficiencies within the child. If she surrounds herself with a hostile environment, then she can change the genetic expression of the fetus to adapt to its physical surroundings. If a mother exposes herself to a healthy, nurturing environment that is full of mental stimulation, she may create a child who is more able to advance his or her understanding due to constant mental stimulation. Similarly, what you expose yourself to transfers the energetic information to whatever vibrational frequency that your body harnesses. The physical body, whether born or unborn, is a conductor of energetic expression based upon its assimilation of vibrational frequency.

Further utilizing this model of cellular expression to evaluate disease within the physical body, you can see how disease or illnesses manifest within the physical body. When you hold on to the emotional energies of past negative experiences, whether it is through physical or emotional trauma, you nurture the growth and development of negative energies to exist within the energy body of the spirit. Repeated negative emotional stimulation of the energy body can trigger pain or cause disease within your physical body. The continual stimulation of the negative energies of anger and non-forgiveness can program normal, healthy functional cells to become irritated, dysfunctional or abnormal. The constant stimulation of negative frequency can theoretically cause these cells to grow erratically and can potentially form cancerous tissue. Cancer is the name for diseases in which normal cells become abnormal and divide without control. Thus, uncontrolled negative energy can translate to uncontrolled negative expression.

When you become extremely angry, you affect the mood and emotions of the people around you. These same people can take on similar emotional expressions of uncontrolled emotions and behavior that in turn adversely affect others around them. When enough negative emotional energy is created, it can impact a large group of people infectiously in the form of riots and acts of violence. The consciousness of the environment changes to support emotional energies of animalistic survival. In August of 2005, a Category 5 hurricane named Katrina swept the Gulf Coast of Louisiana and Mississippi, causing tremendous wind and flood damage to countless counties, cities and homes. Its destruction left hundreds of people dead and millions of people homeless or without power. The collective feelings of helplessness, desperation and the need to survive led to acts of looting, carjacking, rape and murder. The worst of it came when twenty thousand evacuees were housed within the New Orleans Superdome. With sewer and garbage water rising, lack of food and medicine, the living conditions declined rapidly. Reports came in of children with slit throats, women being dragged off and raped, and corpses that were piling up in the basement. The animalistic need of survival is found within all of us when given the right environment and conditions to harbor and support such energies. Your anger can be recognized by others and can affect a group's expression, leading to mayhem and destruction of your surroundings.

Depression is another expression of the physical body when it has an excess of negative input. It is a mental-emotional state characterized by a pessimistic sense of inadequacy and a despondent lack of activity. The result is a lowering of your vibrational energy levels. By allowing this type of vibrational frequency, you lower the functionality of your cells and create non-operative or lesser functioning cells. Your cells may express conditions caused by lack of normal physiological function such as anemia, immunologic or autoimmune diseases. Conditions that take away normal functions of the body can lessen the quality of your life to the point where you no longer want to function or continue to exist. The belief that you are unable to take on responsibility or accountability for your body and your body's interactions with its physical surroundings removes your functionality in the creation of your life. To choose to hold onto the past through blame hinders growth in your life and in all facets of your development. Because life is impermanent, people who choose not to enjoy the experience of their life suffer not only physically and mentally, but spiritually as well.

The illusions you create with your thoughts, beliefs, and emotions about your life history, whether viewed as positive or negative, are simply attachments to your past. A bruised ego can be empowered by the direction of your emotional attachment. This directs your perception and how you live and control your life. When you choose to suffer, you receive an emotional benefit from your decision to hold onto the energies of your emotions. You may feel somehow justified within your suffering and blame.

Experiencing a forceful act, whether it is physical, verbal or mental, is an exchange of energy through your emotions that causes you to act and react. If the force imposed upon you is greater than the mental control of your truth or identity, this force becomes an emotional draining energy through your mental-emotional acknowledgment. If you decide someone has wronged you, and you choose to empower that decision, then you become trapped within the force of its negative expressions. To mask the expression by choosing to identify with being wronged is not a means of resolution, but a backwards step in further empowering your self-righteousness. To hold on to negativity creates negative expression in all facets of life through the creation of judgment that causes spiritual blocks. To acknowledge a wrongful act and empower it through identification, to hold on to it as a demarcation in your life, creates an anchor that holds you back from your spiritual growth. With acceptance of an experience in your life, you acknowledge its presence as necessary for the learning and growth of your spirit. To be able to acknowledge any experience with acceptance accelerates your spiritual unfolding.

Your physical life is a spiritual expression of your level of consciousness. How you respond to your everyday life depicts the level of consciousness where you are resonating spiritually. Your physical life is only temporary. It is only a small expression of your spiritual development within your eternal life. If life is perceived as easy and carefree in the face of any obstacle, it allows an expression of wisdom through many lifetimes of experience. If life is a constant rollercoaster of perceived disaster or emergency, it is a representation of inexperience through many lifetimes. This can be recognized within people at any physical age of development, from infant to elderly. The memory of who you are within your spiritual development is embedded within your spiritual genetic makeup that unfolds your personality, morals, and characteristics. These help define your individual need to attract the necessary lessons and experiences for your spirit's growth.

Two individuals standing next to each other can be extremely different or similar, depending upon the spiritual expression that they hold within their physical bodies. How you react to your physical life is simply a choice of how you want to perceive your life—demanding or carefree? To choose to be accountable for life is to choose the direction of your life and know that there are simply choices to be made. Personal accountability through non-judgmental acceptance of your life situation frees you to choose how to move forward. When you attach emotionally, you blame and resist your life situation, you reject learning opportunities and therefore, life becomes more demanding, chaotic and burdensome. If you don't choose your life, then life will choose for you. Whether you choose to be a part of it or resist it, life is impermanent, constantly changing and evolving. To flow with life is to release any emotional-mental resistance. Life as you perceive it is a reflection of your spiritual development.

Advancing more rapidly in your spiritual growth is simply a choice you make and is something that only you can choose for yourself. The speed of development is monitored by your level of devotion to learning knowledge and understanding within the self. To know the self is to seek the self from within to the point where you trust the self. Misled seekers look outside themselves for direction, because they do not yet trust themselves or their own abilities. To seek development through the self begins with a personal relationship with the self.

The first step is to recognize that you create your own false perceptions, whether you choose to attach to these illusions or remain trusting. The experiences you encounter in life teach you discernment within the level of your understanding. If you stand in the power of your presence, you are not subjected to the manipulation of other people's power or illusions. In this sense, you learn from your experiences and the experiences of those around you. Attachment to perceived failure is only an attachment to your emotionally driven ego.

The next step is to choose to live and be accountable for your life at every level of your existence, for you are a creator of your entire life and how you choose to empower it. Taking on the responsibility of your life and all your decisions and actions removes spiritual roadblocks of judgment. It allows further growth and acceptance to flourish within you. With acceptance of yourself, you learn to accept others around you; this helps to balance your life.

The third step is to ask your higher self for guidance. What is your highest purpose, your highest good for your life's expression in the world? What is your greatest purpose here in the world for all of humankind? How can you serve? Remember that the only right answer for your purpose is that which is right for your spirit.

When you come from a place of humility, service and non-judgment, you become clear in your expression. You are willing to be the clay, molded for creation to take place. When you manifest from non-attachment or non-judgment, you can manifest in any direction you choose. As you draw from your spirit's abundance, your cup overflows in abundance in the presence of servitude of the self. You can then draw more and more energy into yourself. You increase and expand your presence of expression and therefore, raise your own levels of vibration to obtain access to higher levels of consciousness within yourself. As you expand, you receive direction that will guide you to the next level that you desire, whether it comes to you in the form of books, teachers, guides or directly from your higher self. Simply surrendering to who you are in your divinity allows growth without limitations. You raise your vibrations to the levels of divinity and reconnect back to who you were before entering your physical body—pure light.

The first step on the path to becoming enlightened is in understanding your spirit starting from true ground zero. The creation of the spirit, the creation of life, the creation of physical existence all correlates within the awareness of life. Your acceptance of the necessity for each step and experience unfolds and expands your consciousness development. Your spirit portrays itself through consciousness, a beginning that only leads to further growth and awareness at every stage of existence.

When the first seven levels of consciousness are obtained, you are only a part of the way along the journey to integrating the higher self within your physical body. To know something within you does not always mean that you live by its truths. Have you ever been told right from wrong, but still chose to do opposite of what you were told? Have you ever done this simply because you can choose to do so? To choose to experience negative or positive expressions of behavior provides the means of expanding your spiritual dimensions and finding a greater balance in who you are. Prior to the doorway of enlightenment awaits the life lessons within the learning ground of experiencing who you are within your physical existence. Mastery at each level of consciousness allows for development and integration of a fully developed "ego," which then becomes the driving force of your wisdom.

In most prior teachings, you are taught that you are not your ego and that the ego is a mindless form or the desires of the self. This becomes true if the ego is seen as separate from you, a fragmented part of the spirit. The ego then becomes a powerful force within the self that controls your life through the emotional fulfillment of desires. With this separatist view, you have bound your growth to lower levels of consciousness, which is why most people fail in achieving enlightenment. The ego is a part of you. To reject the ego is to reject a part of the self and never allow yourself to be whole. As you integrate the higher self with the physical body, you must raise the levels of all of your parts to equality. When your spiritual higher self, physical middle self and the emotional inner child are unified, balanced and working together, you then become balanced. Your ego doesn't have to decide what is right and what is wrong. In essence, all of your parts become equal and your ego becomes your wisdom in its true form. You become empowered by the self and do not look outside yourself for approval, direction and guidance.

As you integrate and connect each spiritual fragment within the identity of your spirit, you grow energetically with the addition of each energy center of the chakra bodies. The resonation of each chakra fragment, fully connected and resonating, creates the force of your spiritual resonance and human vibration as you master each level of consciousness within yourself. Full mastery of your spiritual fragments allows your spirit to attract growth in what supports your spirit's needs within the physical existence. You emanate your energies outward to attract growth and abundance as your energies integrate with the magnetic energy field of your surroundings. This then aligns you with the higher vibrations of universal consciousness not bound to the lower frequencies of your self-created illusion. You can leave lower realms of survival consciousness and enter into the realm of conscious awareness and acceptance of everything around you. The reward of your divinity is to live life in awareness of everything, harmonizing with the energies around you, the energies that create growth and abundance. Within the achievement of awareness, you then add to your energies and bring forth the spiritual body and unite it with the physical body. This allows you to become the full expression of your spiritual energy, the vibrating force that allows for further understanding within the greater depths of the spiritual and physical experience. This unity holds infinite possibilities and is the very fabric of universal creation. You'll learn more about this as we explore the union of the spirit in the balance of your feminine and masculine energies, the same energies that unite and bring forth the life of your divine spirit.

CHAPTER 15

THE FEMININE
AND MASCULINE

The creation of life begins as being complete. You cannot have
a front without a back. You cannot have a top without a
bottom. You cannot have an outside without an inside. The
creation of existence means to start out as being complete. You are
complete within the physical-spiritual makeup of creation, because
you cannot be physical without all of your spiritual parts. As you enter
any level of existence, whether spiritual or physical, you contain the
essence of divine creation that is waiting to unfold as you continue
your journey. In order to be birthed of divine creation, you must
have the presence of all opposing energies: light and dark, good and
bad, negative and positive, yin and yang, and masculine and feminine.
Opposing energies allow for balance within the many degrees and
dimensions of creation. The opposing energies that create existence
itself are found within the union of the masculine and feminine
energies. The creation of any living species is formed from the union

of masculine and feminine energetic expressions. The presence of both energies within your spiritual makeup roots itself within the balance of existence and survival as a means to support growth and development.

Consider the supporting foundation of creation. Everything starts in the womb of feminine expression. The unborn child is cared for and nurtured within the warmth and protection of the womb, a place where growth, nourishment and development takes place. In entering the physical existence, the same qualities of creation are necessary to support the life of a newborn child. Love, attention, interaction, and patience are the foundations of a healthy relationship between the parent and child. This also provides a positive environment for developing a child's emotional growth, perception and stability, which in turn feeds future personal and professional relationships. These nurturing characteristics allow for creativity and intelligence to develop within the mental mind and perception of a person. The wisdom and truth of your physical and spiritual existence is aligned within the informational energies of the feminine expression. Therefore, as you nurture the growth and development of your spirit within your physical existence, you unfold the innate intelligence of your spirit as you ascend higher levels of truth within you. The knowledge that supports growth and development within your physical and spiritual foundations roots itself within the wisdom of the feminine energies of your spirit.

When nurturing yourself, you begin from a place of caring. The nurturing part of the self is the intelligence of the student and teacher within the feminine aspect of your spirit. At its highest expression, it represents the purest feminine energy within you, the energy that supports and maintains intelligence for the continuation of life. The feminine core of your spirit defines your knowledge, wisdom and direction by giving birth not only to your existence, but to your intelligence and creativity. Without the feminine aspect of creation, there is no birth or life. The creation of life begins with the female energy. The part of you that listens, observes, and nurtures the spirit is found within the feminine aspect of the spirit. The feminine part of you develops the emotional integrity of the inner child and allows for mental and intellectual growth to take place. Within a nurturing environment, you are able to create and manifest at will, but in a forceful or manipulating environment, there is little room to allow for the expansion of creativity that fuels your intelligence.

The maternal instinct resides strongly in the feminine spirit, whether femininity is expressed physically or not. A nurturing ability is found within your feminine expression of your spirit, whether you are physically male or female. To listen to this particular part of yourself is to listen to your feminine maternal instinct which guides your intuition and knowledge of understanding. When you draw from your intellect and creativity, you draw from your femininity. When you come to the realization that you are more than your physical expression, you can achieve balance by utilizing the masculine and feminine parts of yourself equally.

As you enter into your physical existence, you manifest through your masculinity that drives the spirit forward towards survival and protection of its feminine creation. Your animalistic ego takes on the conscious view of the masculine part of you, and takes control of your physical body for its protection. Your masculinity then further defines the boundaries of who you are within the world of survival. Once defined, it becomes the driver for where you are heading in your life. It does this by raising the masculine energy, taking the information of the feminine and then projecting its expression forward into your physical existence. The masculine energy is the driver and the disciplinarian of the spirit. It allows you to define who you are and what you are willing to do to advance and survive. Within the developing consciousness, the masculine is the father figure that motivates and tells you how well or poorly you are doing. It is your self-created consciousness, constantly reminding you to keep going when you fall down, or tells you to get off the bus when the road becomes too bumpy or dangerous.

Socially and historically, the masculine archetype is understood as "the man of the house" or "leader of the pack," the father or provider for the household. It represents the protector of your physical body and human life. Your masculine energy is the provider of your physical existence within the physical world. In days past, it was common for the male of the house to provide for the family and make the majority of household decisions. Men hunted for food, built shelter and offered protection against predators and those who could inflict harm. The same traits of masculine duties have been extended to your physical self, regardless of what you express in gender. Your masculinity helps you stand up for yourself when you are faced with fear, insult, or danger. It motivates the spirit by driving you to achieve or accomplish goals. It also provides a sense of discipline. Where your consciousness lies will determine how you motivate or direct yourself, either by empowering you positively or negatively. It determines whether you take other people's judgments personally or if you are motivated to believe there is nothing that you cannot do or nothing other people can say that will stop you. Your masculinity can be your promoter or inhibitor. We also reference stubbornness or aggressive behaviors as male traits. In essence, your masculinity is the part of you that manifests or creates your inner desires to become your physical realities.

As the world advances, more and more of the masculine and feminine expressions are working equally in individuals and in society. Women are taking on leadership and managerial roles in the business world. Men are staying at home and taking care of the children while women provide the main income for the family. In order for society to advance, so must the equality of masculine and feminine roles. Balancing your own equality provides full expression of the self and your infinite potential. To define yourself limits your ability to achieve. To live within the socially-defined roles of your masculine and feminine traits limits your creative, intellectual, physical, and spiritual evolution. You limit your physical and spiritual potential. Raising your parts equally allows you to learn from your masculine and feminine energies. It permits faster growth of your spirit and the attainment of higher levels of consciousness. When you achieve balance and equality within yourself, it is expressed outwardly in all aspects of your life. You remove the judgments you place upon yourself and therefore remove judgments you place upon others.

It always begins with the self. Until you are able to recognize the self, you are unable to fully express yourself outwardly as a spiritually aligned expression for others to witness. To seek the self is to understand that the only goal you are working toward is found internally and not externally. To know and learn from the self, from spirit, does not give you rewards or notoriety, but is a discovery of that which you are in your entirety. If an engine is missing a part, the engine will not run properly—at least not very efficiently. As you begin to take on all of your fragments at each level of consciousness, you begin to master who and what you truly are. As you acknowledge and accept your fragments at each level of your consciousness, you receive yourself unconditionally. As you advance each level, you learn more and more about who you are and all that you are capable of. In your personal acceptance, you erase lines of false perceptions and judgments that were self-created to begin with. The more you are able to accept yourself as capable and complete, despite your perceived flaws, the more acceptances you have of others. You are no longer dominated by the fear and resistance that creates your self-imposed boundaries. You live and function out of knowing and accepting yourself and everything around you. With less resistance, you become open and connected with everything around you. Being open allows you to synchronize with the energies around you in harmony. Your vibrations empower you to the levels of your truth, the levels of manifestation versus the levels of attachment that create false illusions. You are able to detach from people and events in your life that create mental resistance within your illusions, allowing you to live in the present moment of who you are.

The balance of the masculine and feminine energies working in unison allows a person to be in balance and in acceptance of the self. This allows you to be who you are and to manifest your life without the anchors and attachments to people and events that hold you back from advancing your path. Whether your purpose is to serve, create or invent, you are here to experience yourself, which helps others to experience themselves. Ideally, your experiences will lead to your growth; you achieve this by simply being and accepting who you are and not allowing external things to define you. You define yourself by how you perceive your life experience.

To truly live life is to love life, and the only way you can do this is to love yourself in your entirety. To understand that although you may be an outward expression of the physical body, you are no different than the person who stands next to you on the street or someone who lives in another country. You are equally exposed to the fragments that make up the individual, and you choose where you stand along your karmic path. To take on the accountability of your internal worlds and not blame the world around you for what has been done to you adds to the energies around you. The level of your consciousness gives you the ability to choose how you perceive your experience. Acceptance paves the road to the acceleration of your awareness of who you are. When you blame the world for what happens to you, you are simply blaming yourself. You express a spiritual fragment within yourself. How whole you are determines how much acceptance you allow yourself to achieve and experience. So if you are only an aspect of your wholeness, you can only express the spiritual fragment that you are. When you unite all your fragments and balance all your parts, you give full expression to who you are and become unlimited.

When balanced within your spirit, you work out of the balance of your masculine and feminine energies. The feminine provides your wisdom and nurtures your physical and spiritual self; in essence, your feminine is the spiritual representation of your higher self. Your masculine is the part within you that motivates and drives you to move forward for your spiritual and physical survival. It provides you strength and protection within your physical existence and represents the true power of the human spirit. It stands up for you when you are feeling vulnerable or weak. It is the inner strength within you that allows you to thrive. Without balance within your wisdom and strength, you falsely empower your ego. Whether it is your self-righteousness that blinds you from seeing with clarity and awareness, or your stubbornness that prevents you from seeing your wisdom, life's experiences will eventually teach you how to live in balance within your masculine and feminine energies. Without balance within your own spirit, you hear the internal noise expressed within your mental mind. Enlightenment is simply the balance of all of your energies within you, within all levels of your consciousness. That includes your masculine and feminine parts, which ultimately evolve the ego into your wisdom. Your feminine and masculine parts develop as you develop your consciousness and ascend the levels of enlightenment. With conscious intelligence, power is created in the balance of both energies. Understanding your power lies within the proper development of the ego. Development of the ego evolves into the power of your spiritual wisdom.

CHAPTER 16

TRUE EGO

When people talk about the role of the "ego" in their
spiritual growth, they usually reference it as meaning
something negative or something that holds them back
spiritually. They see this thing called the "ego" as a roadblock on the
path to spiritual awakening and enlightenment. They believe that the
ego prevents them from obtaining higher levels of consciousness and
awareness within themselves. Building on the idea of unconditional
acceptance, not rejection, which is the rule that governs our universal
laws, is it possible that the ego has been misconstrued and misunderstood? Why was the ego created? Why is the ego present within
you as you unfold your spiritual development? Does the ego have
an important purpose in your life rather than being something you
must deny, reject or destroy within you? Why would the ego be the
only part of you that needs rejection or avoidance when the arrows of
higher consciousness point to unconditional love and acceptance?

Let's propose the idea that the ego actually plays an important
role in your spiritual growth and development. Once you understand

the developmental process and the principles behind each chakra body, you will see that the ego is the supporting essence of who you really are. The ego becomes the teacher and mirror that reflects the current state of consciousness that allows you to choose and direct your consciousness growth. It drives and motivates you to learn and master the control of your emotions, your lessons, and your attachment to mental illusions. When you have achieved a level of awareness and understanding within each life lesson, it allows you the choice to let go of the emotional energy around your experience.

Acceptance is the divine will of your spiritual source. The ego was created as the mirror of your consciousness by showing you the degree of resistance you are creating. You can recognize your ego expressing itself when you feel any degree of resistance within you as you experience life. Resistance is any negative feeling you encounter: an emotional irritation about someone or some experience you perceive as having insulted you, hurt you, humiliated you, and so on. The scale of negative or resistant emotions and reactions can range from mild irritation to deep emotional anger, pain, and fear.

Have you ever taken a class, perhaps a new language, a new skill, a new area of study that you felt would improve or add to your existing skills or profession? Have you ever started a class completely frustrated, or have moments of anger or confusion because you found it hard to grasp the concepts being taught? After these moments of resistance, you suddenly have a mental shift where something clicks and all the bits and pieces of information come together as you reach a point of clarity. In essence, the ego is the teacher of your conscious awareness, a reflection or sounding board within the development of your consciousness. It is the part of you that reflects those separated pieces of information about your consciousness evolvement and directs your learning process through your thoughts and emotions. This helps remind you to utilize the information that makes up who you are along the way to clarity. When you feel resistance, this is the ego reminding you of the lessons still needing to be learned and overcome to achieve clarity. Only with unconditional acceptance can you achieve total clarity and freedom for unlimited spiritual growth and expression.

What holds you back most within your spiritual growth? It is the emotional scars created from your experiences that cause energetic ripples within your stream of consciousness and become anchors that slow down your growth. Emotional scars are sometimes deep and unresolved resistance embedded within your spiritual energy field. These emotional anchors remind you of past life and present life experiences that have not been energetically resolved. Unresolved emotional experiences can affect your spiritual development and create mental-emotional instability and lack of control. The emotional scars you hold onto and empower through the memory of your thoughts disrupt and distort your spiritual energy. Stimulating these energetic blocks slows your development of spiritual consciousness.

Through your thoughts and emotions, you create energetic spikes within your energy body that can prevent you from receiving and assimilating energy around you. Spikes within your energy are similar to rocks in riverbeds. The larger the rock, the more the water diverts its stream and flow. When water flow increases, the large rock creates turbulence within the flowing stream. Similarly, when you increase your mental-emotional energy, your emotional scars create turbulence and resistance within your stream of consciousness. When you are able to find a way to release emotional scars, you remove the block of energy flow. This is usually done by your spirit as it attracts and repeats similar emotional experiences that, when recognized, understood and accepted, allow you to reach clarity. You are then able to release the energies of your mental and emotional scars that slow your spiritual growth.

The ego points out the open emotional wounds that you need to address by expressing feelings of resistance within you, while motivating you to overcome these experiences and move forward in life. The ego also evolves with you as your consciousness evolves, until it becomes the strength of your wisdom within the knowledge of experiences and awareness of your potential. At the highest levels of consciousness, you no longer resist but accept your life experience as lessons for growth, and you self-motivate to understand and learn; thus, your ego has evolved into your wisdom.

Throughout history, the ego has been rejected and misunderstood, because the level of consciousness within society was less developed. As consciousness evolved, a higher form of intelligence has allowed society to advance. Humanity has outgrown the consciousness level of its past. Therefore, your understanding of the ego must change in order to for you to achieve your spiritual potential.

When you entered your physical body to begin your life experiences, you were initially fully aware of both your physical and spiritual existence. As you transitioned from a place of unconditional awareness within spiritual existence to one that is governed by the consciousness of your physical surroundings, you adapted into your existence at the level of the animalistic ego and human survival. From infancy to adulthood, you evolve physically and consciously. As you evolve, you are developing and unfolding your spirit. You are unfolding who you are spiritually as you ascend levels of consciousness within yourself through the physical experience. As you evolve, you continually test the boundaries of your environment through your choices and actions. In return, the information that you accumulate directs the speed of your growth and maturity, both mentally and spiritually. You grow and develop your ego as you gain levels of consciousness and acceptance within you.

At lower levels of consciousness, the ego presents itself in survival mode for you to function, learn and adapt within your physical environment. In the first part of your life, you are in a mode of acquiring knowledge and experience. Depending upon your environmental support, be it nurturing or challenging, you mold your life through the experience of your upbringing. What you learn and experience helps you to function and advance within your physical environment. This survival instinct continues to harness and control your life until you come to a point where you no longer feel the need to be parented by your social environment. You gain a power of self-worth within yourself; this is your identity and ego strength. When you come to an understanding and are no longer dependent upon your survival instinct to gain validation in your life, you begin to acknowledge yourself from within. This acknowledgment comes as you advance your levels of consciousness until you are able to raise the strength of your spiritual energies to an equal or higher resonation than the energy field of your environment. You create an overflowing sense of balance and fulfillment within you. Lack of self-worth creates a need to identify with the vibrational lack or imbalance of energy within your spirit. Your ego teaches you how to fill the lack of energy in your spiritual resonation.

When you feel a sense of lack in your life—perhaps through coveting material objects, people or wealth, all of which are false representations of who you are—your ego makes sure you recognize it. It does this by attaching to your mental focus of emotional energy and the distortions of energetic balance within your spiritual fragments. This causes fear or resistance, creating a sense of lack or low self-worth, a feeling from within. The true purpose of these emotions is for you to identify and be able to correct and raise your energies back into balance. The best you can do for your growth is to witness and understand your emotions, not to simply experience or be controlled by them. When you balance your energies by changing your internal perspectives, beliefs and emotions, you correct the perceived lack within your life. Remember that you have the ability to empower your choices to change your perspective with any experience. Empowering your choices through the way you understand and perceive your emotional attachments allows you to direct and balance your energies. When you empower your energies by attaching your mental-emotional focus to something external, it causes you to lose strength within yourself as you give your own energy away.

When a child is not receiving attention or love, they react adversely. Children show emotions of anger or sadness and are usually soothed by receiving love and attention. Similar to any other child, your inner child directs your controlled or uncontrolled emotions. When you attach adversely to your experiences, you react from your inner child. It is your unconscious self that causes you to remain emotionally stuck in your lower levels of emotional consciousness. If you are able to learn and grow from your experiences and thus raise your energy from within, you empower yourself from the uncontrolled subconscious level to a conscious level of choice. You develop your conscious intellect to let go of and lessen emotional attachments in your life.

Unfortunately, many people grow up physically, but do not progress the development of their inner child—the keeper of the emotional body. Not confronting and resolving past issues of fear, denial or rejection from an emotional standpoint causes energetic emotional scaring of the spirit that you experienced at a young age and from previous lifetimes. This unresolved emotional energy within you follows you into adulthood. This causes you not to be able to understand, accept or forgive yourself or the people and experiences you perceive to have caused you pain. By not recognizing the emotional scarring that the inner child holds onto within you, you continue to allow your inner child to emotionally suffer.

When you become dependent upon outside sources to fill a sense of lack or imbalance from within, you are constantly in need of replacing the imbalance of energies within you. The person that you hope will complete you as a human being replaces a lack of energetic balance that you do not recognize or identify within your own spirit. What happens when the person that you believe completes you leaves? The pain and anguish left behind is the energetic void that you still have to develop and mature within yourself in order for you to become complete and independent. Until this happens, you become dependent on outward attachments, feeding off those energies in order to feel balanced or complete. When you feel empty inside or feel lack in your life, you chase after objects, people and experiences to fill this void.

The replacement of temporary energy is never enough, because it is transient energy that needs to be continually replaced until you can create the same energy within yourself. Because of this constant turnover in the fulfillment of your wants or desires, what you acquire or conquer is stored or thrown away like an old toy after you tire of it, and you move on to the next experience or exchange, trying in vain to find what will fulfill your desires. You begin to seek another substitute to fill your voids and temporarily fill the imbalance. If you suffer from low self-worth, lowered energy, you may compensate outwardly by buying a little something for yourself that might make you feel good. Whether it is spoiling yourself with a delicious treat or a new outfit, spending money to make yourself feel good is utilizing outward attachments of fulfillment that offer only temporary emotional relief to the problem that exists inside you. Until you are ready to deal with the source of the problem, the need to feel good creates continuous attachments for your mind. The need for fulfillment is the idea that you are not already enough to yourself. You are not complete. The truth is that you create your self-perceptions based upon your need of outward attachments, a temporary fix for feeling fulfillment within yourself.

Not raising your spiritual energies to balance out this energetic imbalance leaves you to constantly struggle between your ego and the mental attachments of your false illusions and identity. Not understanding the difference between the ego and your attachments allows for misrepresentation of the ego. The ego feeds on emotional energy, but that is only part of the story. The ego empowers itself when your spiritual energies are out of balance. The resulting imbalance of energies creates spikes and lulls within your energy field that identifies with your conscious middle or physical self. This is your ego telling you to wake up when you are not in balance. The ego monitors the energetic balance of your spirit by making you aware of your energetic imbalance, your degrees of resistance. The wisdom learned within your physical and spiritual consciousness is comprised of the experiences that you have and the information that you gather, allowing you to bring your energies back into balance and stability.

The main function of your ego is to assist your spiritual evolvement by helping you to identify and recognize where you are in your spiritual growth through your degrees of resistance and acceptance. It initially acts like an alarm, ringing when you are out of balance, and later it becomes the light of your wisdom as you grow. The ego reflects the mirrored light of your current spiritual development, offering you glimpses into your overall consciousness at the present moment. How you react to the events that take place within your life depends on how you attach to your environment. Where you are in your spiritual growth affects your understanding and acceptance of your surroundings, which are in turn influenced by your conditioned social upbringing. Rejecting various parts of yourself leads to the rejection of your surroundings and causes you to seek a source of fulfillment or empowerment outside yourself. This takes away from your energies, energies you need in order to balance your spirit and its spiritual fragments working together as one powerful force.

When you feed off your attachments to feel fulfilled within one or more aspects of your spiritual makeup, you cause imbalance in your energies and begin to create separation within the self. The internal noises that consume your thoughts are the separate voices of each spiritual fragment. Depending on how strong your attachment is to the outer world, you empower various fragments of your spirit to create separate identities within your mental self. These empowered energies begin to war for survival within the self, trying to dominate and control your thoughts and the reactions of your physical body. Each level of consciousness is a separate energy center with a specific role or function for the growth and development of your consciousness. If you continually stimulate one spiritual fragment more than the rest, it creates a separate identity within the physical body. At first, it could be the rationale of your own conscious behavior creating thoughts like, "Did I do well? Yes? Was I good enough? Maybe I wasn't good enough? Maybe I could have done more? Maybe I was terrible or did a bad thing?" These are conscious questions that are stimulated within various levels of consciousness within the chakra bodies. When one fragment is more stimulated than the others over a long period of time, it can result in split or multiple personalities within your consciousness.

Multiple personalities are a rare condition caused by the absence of a clear and comprehensive identity; they are an exaggerated state of what occurs when your spiritual fragments are over-stimulated and out of balance. In most cases, two or more independent and distinct personality systems develop in the same individual, as he or she over-stimulates a spiritual fragment and gives it more energy or power. Each personality may alternately inhabit the person's conscious awareness to the exclusion of the others, but one is usually dominant. The various personalities within each chakra body differ from one another as they express at different levels of consciousness evolvement. This condition results from the splitting of conscious awareness and separated control of your thoughts, feelings, and memories. These mental components are emotional energetic responses to situations that are painful, disturbing, or somehow unacceptable to the person experiencing them. The empowerment of separated fragments within your spirit results in a sense of imbalance in your own energies, a rejection of various parts of the spiritual self. Not accepting yourself in your entirety causes further fragmentation of your spiritual makeup, making it harder for you to balance and raise the level of your spiritual vibrations equally in order to advance your consciousness. The existence of multiple personalities or identities within a person further reinforces the fact that your physical body is merely a shell for various resonations of spiritual energies to exist. These separated energies are the vibrations of your spiritual fragments. You are not your thoughts, but you *are* the energies of your spirit that remain separated until you are able to unify your fragments and become spiritually whole.

If you constantly empower the outside world to measure your value, you overcompensate by buying into material identities to validate you. You may try to acquire a social status that will mask your lack of self-esteem. You find yourself constantly trying to satisfy other people's perceptions and approval, choosing situations that limit your spiritual growth. If I do *this*, then I get *that*. If I have *this*, then people will believe that I am *that*. You constantly play mental games, trying to fill a bottomless barrel. In this manner, you will never reach your goal because the outside world is forever changing. The illusionary world constantly takes from all who want to give in to its illusion.

When you feel a sense of lack within yourself, it not only affects you but the relationships that support you. If you look at the ego in terms of personal relationships, you can see why so many people become dependent on others to balance their energies. As you enter into a relationship, you begin to combine and integrate two separate energies fields. With the addition of new energies from your partner, you are given the choice of expanding your own energies or staying complacent. With the expansion of your energies, you become a little disarrayed at first and therefore your energies become heightened and you enter into what some people call "the honeymoon phase" of a relationship. Increased energy conveys increased stimulation or excitement. When two people begin to discover and integrate a balance between both energies, new energy translates to love. As you take on and integrate these new energies, you may adapt the voice of your partner or your partner's consciousness resonation. You learn and experience the different aspects of your vibrations in relation to their consciousness resonation, the things that identify and represent you and the things that you lack within your own energy field.

This exchange of energies conveys itself within both parties. The dominant energy field of you or your partner may cause you to overcompensate your own ideals or actions to mimic the needs or desires of your partner. For example, if your new partner is still healing from the emotional scars of separation, divorce or adultery, the coddling of her emotions may dictate the initial direction and comfort level of the relationship until the two of you find trust and balance. As you integrate the energies shared between two individuals, you begin to either fuse or repel one another in the attempt to find stability of both energies. After the integration has settled, you see whether these new energies are enough for you to hold and maintain a beneficial relationship. Either the energies will benefit and complement each other, or you will find yourself seeking outside of that relationship for fulfillment. This cycle repeats itself until you are balanced and fulfilled within yourself. You no longer are dependent on someone else's energy to fulfill the desire for love and happiness.

By viewing relationships in terms of external empowerment, whether they are personal or professional, you see that two people initially come together out of a level of benefit or gain. When both parties are in agreement, they thrive on shared energies until the agreement is satisfied or fulfilled. Sometimes when the level of benefit from one party outweighs the benefit received from another, you tend to lean toward ending your agreement and moving onto the next. If you stay within the imbalance of energies, you begin to harness negative energies that may lead to negative outcomes. Resentment, anger, or other forms of lower level emotions can lessen the energies of both parties, taking away from one another instead of adding to one another. If you do not sacrifice your own energies to support lower energies outside of you, you are able to start at a functional state of existence rather than harbor negative accumulated attachments that may create ill will toward others.

From these examples of energy exchanges between two individuals, notice that there is a resemblance to how you balance your own energies, whether they are drawn from your inner or outer worlds. When you see a perceived lack within you, you often attach to other sources of energies to balance out your own deficiencies. If you take an internal approach to raising your energies by first recognizing and accepting where you are in your spiritual development, you can then begin to empower your deficiencies. You begin to recognize and acknowledge the emotional problems that continually arise. If you dislike a person, ask yourself why. If you dislike your relationship, ask yourself why. If you dislike your job, ask yourself why. Instead of seeking an answer that blames, ask yourself how it relates to you and how can you resolve this within yourself. If you can find the strength to answer these questions and follow through with what is right for you, you no longer have to depend upon outside sources to support your world and the way you interact and perceive yourself. You can then work from your own power, by detaching from your false perceptions and identities of yourself towards a place of no self. You can equalize your own spiritual energy and work on raising your energies in balance. This is how you come to enjoy the presence of others without attaching to the idea that they must fulfill your emotional needs.

When you reject certain aspects of yourself, you fragment your spirit and leave a part of yourself behind, creating imbalance within your energies. Not raising your fragments equally makes it harder to advance. You remain stuck in your current surroundings or situations, repeating the lessons or experiences until you have come to balance and accept yourself in your entirety. When you are able to empower the spirit equally rather than the individual fragments of yourself, you can leave behind the attachments that continually reappear in different manifestations in your life. Empowering individual fragments of the spirit to hold onto the past takes more energy to maintain. Even if you do not recognize or empower the parts of you that are rejected, if they are left unattended, you allow these parts to take on their own identities and become false representations within your spirit. They are mental anchors of past experiences. When you live in acceptance of the present, you are vibrationally balanced within your spirit.

Everything that you empower within your spirit has its own way of eventually balancing itself. When you don't accept various aspects of your life and fail to take on the responsibility of the environment that you create, you separate yourself spiritually. You begin to bicker with yourself internally. Blame and resentment keep you energetically attached to lower-level energies of negativity within the self. In essence, everything you do, you do with intent, consciously or unconsciously; either way, it creates a conscious decision to act. When you do not want to accept the actions of your intent, you can mentally talk yourself in every single direction until you finally come into acceptance within yourself. Within acceptance, you create the ability to move forward. Without resolution and acceptance within yourself, you leave a part of you in the past. It remains there as a reminder that you still have work to do, in order to balance the spirit.

No one else chooses your experiences in life. You choose the experiences for yourself that you focus on and mentally attach to. If it is an experience you believe to be an accident or one that you would never consciously choose, then it is one of your spirit's choosing and you are simply not consciously aware of it. Every life experience exists for you to learn and grow. When you reject your own actions and identify yourself as a victim to life's experiences, you create a false identity within your energy field; you choose to continually empower this experience through your resistance. It remains there until you have resolved it within yourself. Some people call this your subconscious, but it is simply a mental reminder of what you still need to work on in order to stop attracting the lessons that you self-created.

Every single aspect of your life is self-governed, but not over-looked by your higher self and the universe in which it interacts. To perform perceived good or bad acts causes a positive or negative energy exchange, one that enhances or depletes from the energies of your surroundings. What you take from your surroundings is energetically repaid in one form or another. What you take from your external energies, you exchange with your own. If you constantly cause physical or verbal abuse—an exchange of negative energy—people can sense that in your physical presence. The creation of negative energy creates negative expression within your demeanor. In sensing your negative energy, people may choose not to interact or support your physical or spiritual growth. Negative expression can cause you to appear to be uncooperative, useless or problematic. People may not want to place the energy of their efforts in supporting you. The result of your negative actions can cause you to remain jobless, unemployed and angry at the world. You cause your life to become stuck and experience a stall in your mental and spiritual growth.

When you add to the energies of your environment with the will of your highest intent, you attract positive outcomes or events. The positive energy of your intent continually projects you forward along your growth. Your energies become abundantly overflowing through the impact of your positive expression, which allows you to attract choices in infinite directions and infinite possibilities.

Simply observing your internal thoughts allows you to measure where you are in your spiritual development. Observe the voice of your ego and what it is trying to tell you about your own consciousness. The more fragmented your spirit is, the more there is separation within your mental self, which causes internal emotional conflict—a war between the fragments of the spirit. This internal conflict causes disruption and creates internal noise, the same noise that most religions and philosophies direct you to reject as the misunderstood ego. By attaching to your internal voices (separated spiritual fragments), you empower separation and become the "experiencer" of your mental-emotional attachments. To simply observe your internal voices without judgment gives you understanding and direction as to where you are in your consciousness development and where you need to redirect yourself. You remain the "watcher" or "witness" when experiencing your ego. If you continually look outside yourself, you create a false identity within the self. You continue to chase an illusion instead of looking for and seeing the self.

You cannot help yourself until you choose to do so by re-engaging your spirit. The higher self of your spirit watches over you and tries to help and direct you, only intervening when it sees you are at a place where you choose to be helped. The higher self has no problem allowing you to choose suffering and destruction, simply because you no longer choose to be a part of your own solutions. If you choose to seek help outwardly, you can only be helped to the level of which you are willing to accept within yourself. You need to consciously parent the fragments that make up your whole spiritual makeup, until you reunite all the fragments of your complete self.

The ego can be viewed as your greatest teacher—or your greatest enemy if you choose to war against yourself. For who knows *you* better than you? Causing separation within yourself allows for disruption in your life and impedes the growth of your spirit. If you treat yourself as a victim, then you have enslaved your growth to the energetic deficiencies of your past. In doing so, you can affect your present and future spiritual growth adversely.

Attaching to anything other than who you are causes a disruption in your growth and results in a separation within the self. Separation within the self lowers your vibration, causing you to separate from your spirit and hindering your growth and development. Just like any group or nation, if you do not allow all the pieces to come together and function as a successful entity, you impede progress and advancement at all levels of your success. A highly efficient person, group, business, or community adds to the wealth of their environment. You must look at yourself as a successful partnership among all of your spiritual fragments. In so doing, you add to your environment through the vibration of who you are in the power and wisdom of your ego. To choose to accept the wisdom of all that you are unlocks the unlimited potential of your spirit.

How do you best free yourself from resistance and learn to be better guided by your wisdom, which is the highest expression of your ego? The next chapter will show you how, by adding the power of knowing your own free will within the totality of who you are. You can choose to take one step closer to freeing yourself from your own attachments and allow yourself to be you.

CHAPTER 17

FREE WILL

E veryone in this world cherishes his or her personal freedom and the ability to evoke their "free will." We like to think that we are in complete control of our lives, our minds and our bodies to do just about anything and everything that we want or desire, assuming we have the means to. But what means do we actually have? What means are we capable of? And why is it that not everyone in this world is living out their dreams, wishes, or desires if we have the means and free will? How much control of your life or your reality do you really have? The truth is that your free will is not all that free when viewed from the perspective of the development of your physical and spiritual consciousness. It is your level of consciousness, your ability to understand and interact within the energy fields of manifestation, the energies within the laws of attraction that dictate the probability of you manifesting your success or goal in life.

Answering simple questions can show you where you are in your own consciousness development and understanding. Do you think your feelings and emotions dictate your truth and reality? Do you think that your perception and understanding of the world around you is reality? Do you think that this life and everything you experience is your reality? If this is true, then ask yourself if your understanding, perceptions and your reality were the same for you five or ten years ago? Is your reality the same for you after being married, separated, or divorced? Is it the same for you after having your first child, second child, or experiencing the inability to bear children? Your mental realities change as your life changes, as you experience and grow into wisdom and understanding through the experiences that make up your life. From your initial learning to mastering any knowledge, skill or wisdom, you go from resistance to effortless thought.

If it seems hard to grasp this concept, then ask yourself what becomes of your reality when you pass from this life to whatever awaits you on the other side. Ask yourself, "How can I be free if I am a prisoner or slave to my mental mind?" The need to feel in control causes your mind to focus and attach to the mental illusion of your experience. The power of your attachments, the illusions and emotions that you create that attach to your mental perceptions of reality are extremely powerful. Your mental attachments can control and mold your perceptions of a constantly changing reality. Your attachments control how you perceive your life.

Have you ever fallen in love with someone at work, at school, or someone you just met in a restaurant, bar, or on the street? Your interaction or experience with them makes you feel that you have established this undeniable connection, attraction, closeness, or bond. You find yourself asking the other person whether he or she feels the same connection in hopes of taking things a step further, a level beyond acquaintance or friendship. What if the response you get is rejection? "No, I do not feel the same way." What happened to this feeling, this undeniable truth that you felt was real? These are stories you can create to tell yourself that because you feel, this must be real. The only free will that you have is the freedom to create your own mental perceptions, illusions, and feelings that tell you where you are in your consciousness development. This is the ability to know and choose fiction from reality.

In fact, you really have no real free will at all. You have only choices and even your choices are not always of your choosing, but set for you by your higher consciousness. The experiences resulting from your choices add to the wisdom of your higher intelligence, to be used in the development of the spirit. Take for example, two different people, Susan and John, each fired from their jobs. Unable to comprehend why his employer would throw him to the wayside after 15 years of loyal service, John is blinded by anger, shame and deep feelings of victimization. He spends many months being unemployed and feeling depressed. Susan, on the other hand, takes time to evaluate the situation and decides that it is a chance for her to try something different. She takes the situation as a challenge and uses her severance pay to fund some classes and start her own business, discovering parts of herself she never before imagined. These are examples of similar situations with different levels of attachments that create different actions based upon where an individual is within his or her level of consciousness.

The one thing that is truly considered free is the freedom and choice of perception. Since you are the actor and director in a major motion picture called "life," you get to choose how you want to perceive the experience based upon where you are in your conscious awareness.

So what does this "free will" really mean? Let's look at how you start the day. When the alarm goes off, you choose whether to get straight out of bed or take additional time to snooze. You begin to map out your day based upon a multitude of choices that you choose to entertain. Whatever you decide to do begins to illustrate and evoke different scenes and experiences that you choose to attract and engage. You decide whether to go to work, go to school, or do nothing at all. The simple act of doing nothing is still doing *something*. Meanwhile, the clock continues to tick and time keeps moving while you prepare to make decisions. You are, in essence, harnessing your energies to engage within the world, the energy field of your environment. You make a choice to go to work, but what happens when you get to work is most likely out of your control. You made a choice, but the results of this choice are not within your complete control. To engage in the flow of your life experiences through unconditional acceptance of the outcome allows you to further advance the understanding of yourself. Your ability to choose to enact your "free will" is the ability to choose your perceptions and attachments that help you learn and grow consciously from the creations of your mental illusions.

What we call life is thus an ever-changing invitation that stops for nothing and no one. Every second that passes, an unimaginable number of events take place, noticed and unnoticed. Every day, new life begins and other lives end. Some people are lying on the beach soaking up the sun while others are huddled near a fire, bundled up to keep themselves from freezing to death. Parts of the Earth may be experiencing natural disasters, while others remain calm and pristine. An incredible flux and multitude of interactions and occurrences.

Now, put yourself within this flurry of activity. You are a minute spec on a thread within this web of consciousness. Ask yourself if you are choosing life or is life choosing you. What is the purpose of your false sense and need to feel like you are in control of your day? What energies do you exhaust by trying to force control within your life or the lives of others through your thoughts and actions? All the while, this immense web of activity occurs all around you and beyond you. What if, prior to your physical existence, your spirit made these life choices for you?

Looking at what takes place within the creation of your experiences, you can see that millions of things occur continuously all around you. One morning, you walk down the street and you may see dozens of people but take no notice of any of them, because you are so focused on your own thoughts. If you sit down and talk to a friend, you may become so engrossed in your conversation that you ignore the many other people milling around. But what happens if, all of the sudden, two cars collide on a street nearby? You might stop to react for a brief second, you might choose to assist anyone hurt in the collision, or you may decide simply to continue on with your day. Do the mental or physical interactions and energies of the experience affect your day? Do you end up feeling great because you helped a person that was harmed in the event? Did it not even register within your field of awareness, because you were so engrossed by the topic of conversation between you and your friend? During just a short morning, you were exposed to a myriad of events and experiences, few of which were within your direct control. You have the freedom to choose where to focus your attention and what to ignore. You have a choice of how you attach to each experience presented to your thoughts and emotions.

One spring morning, James decided to go for a ride on his motorcycle. It had been a long and snowy winter. He couldn't wait to enjoy the hills. Deciding to take a route that was new to him, he started on his journey. Suddenly, a car veered in front of him. A shocking accident ensued and James was left with a smashed bike, a severely broken leg, a few cracked ribs and several months in the hospital for recovery and rehabilitation. James made a harmless choice that morning to enjoy doing one of the things that he loved most, riding his motorcycle. James could never have predicted or controlled the events that took place after he made the decision to enjoy his life. How will he handle the experience? How will it impact his life? Will he live in darkness, blame and fear? Or will he learn to value every precious moment of his life afterward?

Any choice you make brings another set of choices for you to consider, and the results can affect you vibrationally. A drop of water can create the smallest ripple on a calm pond, but the amount of splashing and kicking, the amount of emotional waves you provide your mental mind can create larger and larger waves within your stream of consciousness. The way you stimulate mental attachments within your consciousness will allow the experience to either remain with you for a short period of time or for many years to come, depending on the size of the emotional ripple. What is important is not so much the event or experience, but how you perceive and attach to the experience. It is about how quickly you are able to process or learn from the experience, and then let it go to move on to the next learning experience. This is what allows you to grow. When you attach to the experience and hold onto the energy of the experience, you continually feed it more and more energy to keep it alive in your consciousness. This causes you to continually attach to the energies of the emotions surrounding that event and forces you to remember—making you a slave to the power of your emotional attachment.

Let's evaluate how attachment works from an energetic perspective. When you acknowledge various energy forms, you empower them to exist within your mental environment. You empower them by attaching energetically to what you choose to identify with, whether it is perceived by you as positive or negative. Your mental recognition gives this energy form and power to create identity, validation and existence through the emotional energy you place on it. When doing so, you resonate the positive or negative emotional energies of your attachments that you place on your experiences. These powerful emotional energies can anchor into your consciousness, and if allowed to remain present, can then affect the rest of your day, life, or lifetimes. It creates karmic existence through your repeated thoughts, actions, and emotions that fuel the emotional identity of your past. These emotional anchors burden and limit the growth and development of your consciousness and your spirit.

Have you ever been praised for an achievement or award? The emotional high that you receive fuels the momentum for you to go celebrate and continue to do more in your life. Have you ever been told that you were wrong? Depending on what resistant energies you engage, the experience can cause you to react positively or negatively in many ways. If positive, you look for solutions and resolution. If negative, you may become angry and defensive, creating mental scenarios of what-ifs and maybes, all which usually result in an imaginary illusion of negativity, violence or confrontation. You become a vessel for different energies to exist within you and express through your physical body. Depending on how much you empower these energies, it can express into your physical existence.

Remember that you are, in essence, energy that vibrates at different levels of frequencies, based on your current level of conscious awareness and understanding. As well, everything around you holds different levels of consciousness energy. It is important to keep in mind that even though you cannot physically see or experience something, it can still exist. Think of how you memorize things. To remember something is to try to recreate it visually in your mental mind. To be able to remember a fact, a name, or a person means that it is energetically rooted with an emotional attachment to what you are trying to remember. The greater the emotional charge, whether experienced through charged emotions or through repetition, the greater the degree of energy that attaches the memory to your mental energy field.

To remember all the people that walk by you everyday would be hard to do. The one person that bumps into you by accident begins to register within your energy field. The one person that bumps into you and causes you to spill your hot cup of coffee registers a little more. The same person bumps into you and apologizes, but you decide to react angrily towards the incident, which in turn causes them to react defensively. This energy exchange becomes completely registered within the emotional energy field of your memory. The elevated degree of emotional energy causes you to remain negatively tied to the anger of your experience. This may then affect a part of your day or longer.

To remember an exact experience, you must increase its significance within the mental energy field by applying more emotional energy. To think back to what you did yesterday may be a simple task, but to remember what you did last week or a year ago is much more difficult. Once you have created an energy field that has been accepted or embedded in your memory, you then choose how long you want to hold onto a specific energy within your memory bank of experiences. You have no ready means of easily going back in time to replay the exact events of your past. The only means you have is through the mental energy of your mind, to energetically re-member by re-associating the energy of your spirit within your mind. You can try to recreate or mimic past experiences, but the best you would come up with would be another separate event. You cannot relive any experience, but you can continually relive your emotional-mental record of the experience until you learn to understand, accept, and finally let go of your own resistance.

The law of thermodynamics says that energy can be changed from one form to another but it cannot be created or destroyed. The total amount of energy and matter in the universe remains constant, merely changing from one form to another. In essence, energy can only be converted from one form into another. The exchange of your energies is exchanged with the energy field of your environment. You add emotional energies to the things that you attach to that you perceive as meaningful, increasing the vibrations of energy in your experiences. Whether it is joy, pain, anger, sadness or fear, you are simply energetically reinforcing your attachments to whatever experiences you have chosen to encounter. You energetically attach to the energy field of your environment in order to create the illusion of your experiences. In other words, you create the illusion of your own experience through the lens of your perception.

Given all the choices you make each day, you might now ask yourself, "Isn't this really free will?" To some, the answer may still be yes. Everything you choose to do, you are fully accountable for up to the extent of your chosen actions. But the results or consequences are independent of your choices. Since you cannot know what may happen, you cannot control the people, places or things that are within your environment. You can only energetically influence your environment, but it still has a mind of its own. It continues to move, whether you move with it or not.

When you attach to negative events that have taken place in the past, you leave a part of yourself and your energies in the past. You are most likely to do this with the experience of events that you perceive to be tragic and wrongful acts against you or someone close to you. Since you are choosing to perceive them negatively, the negative energies you attach to can continually drain from you. You drain your own energies by continually acknowledging the memories or encountering similar acts or experiences. This creating and harnessing of negative attraction to a past experience stalls the spiritual, mental, and physical growth in all aspects of your life. Do not consider your experience of a perceived wrongful act as something you do or do not deserve. Instead, realize that when you become aware of your choices, you alone are accountable for you.

Everyone likes to have an opinion on just about anything and everything. It is everyone's right to have an opinion based upon their level of conscious understanding. They are right at their level of understanding, but it does not mean that they are right at *your* level of understanding. Therefore you can only be accountable for you and your actions. The energies of the environment around you are independent variables differentiated from you. By acknowledging and accepting the consequences of choices in your past, you can move forward in the realization that what has happened in the past cannot be changed and that you have learned from the experience. You can either choose to improve yourself and your environment or continue to allow it to take from you. The choice of holding onto the past is simply for your personal validation, empowering selfishness and stalling your growth.

When you empower an experience with positive energies, it adds to you, your environment, and the people around you. You move forward with increased interest and energy. You feel good about yourself and your life. The energy of feeling good is positive forward motion, and your joyful thoughts add to the energies that radiate into your outer worlds. A good memory momentarily energizes you by placing a smile upon your face and joy within your heart. Happiness generates good energies in you and the people around you. When positive energies flow from you, your outlook and your life are viewed in abundance, and attraction radiates in every direction. If you take this concept and apply it to acceptance and forgiveness of your past negative experience, you are able to heal and unplug from the negative energies of the past.

When you feel the need to be justified or acknowledged through the energies you hold on to, be they negative or positive expressions, you are simply telling yourself that you are not enough and are not strong enough to be responsible for yourself. When you need to boast of your achievements or emphasize the victimization of what you have experienced, you are seeking attention within yourself and within your life. To say that what you have chosen to experience is not of your doing indicates that you are not in acceptance of your own life, but victim of life itself. It means you believe that the choices you make are not really who you are and that you are a slave to other people's choices. You believe that someone else is choosing to make you suffer. Victimization is a prime example of being a prisoner to your outer worlds.

If you perceive yourself as a victim, the suggestion that you choose your own suffering may sound ridiculous. But if you apply it to your choice to attach and hold onto negative experiences, you are able to choose how long you need to experience negativity within yourself. No one has chosen to make you suffer except you. You hold onto and relive negative emotions of past experiences rather than striving for acceptance and understanding. Choosing to suffer is a personal decision. Attaching to these energies is similar to inviting another energy form to co-exist within the body. This becomes an energetic pain body to replace the lack of empowerment within you. You fill the void with the energy of your created energetic pain body. Choosing to be a victim allows people or things to take energy away from you, for the energetic pain body is empowered by draining energy from you. You reduce your own energies by allowing yourself to think you are dependent on the void that you have allowed to co-exist within your body. In doing so, you acknowledge that who you are is not enough and that you falsely need whatever it is to represent, identify or validate you, leaving you divided and separated from your actual ability to survive.

If we look at all the catastrophes that have taken place on Earth, no matter how great the perceived loss or gain to Earth or to humankind, we can see that Earth still moves forward in unconditional acceptance of what has happened. Our planet does not stop for a moment to place judgment or stall growth. Whether we have desecrated or rearranged the topography of the land by building our houses, skyscrapers and cities, drilling for oil or mining for gold and precious metals, Earth continues to exist and move forward. It does not look back or attach to the destruction that has taken place in the advancement of human evolution and personal gain. It does not stop to point a finger or ask, "Who did this to me and why did this happen?" It does not say, "Oh, how they have wronged me," simply because Mother Earth is the womb that allows us to experience our own creation. Let Earth be a symbol that accepts and continues to support the existence of all life, all things that exists at every level of consciousness growth and flow.

To attach to your perceived lack slows your growth, preventing growth from coming to you in its fullest expression. Why? Because the world that you have chosen to live in is comprised of your temporary perceived realities. When you come into this world, you experience survival in its most basic form. When you add to this your attachments and false needs, you create illusions about what will bring you happiness and make you complete in your eyes and the eyes of others. Your mental mind inputs what you want versus what you really need. The more that you don't identify with your true self, the more you will want in order to compensate for the lack of acknowledgment within you. You invent things to chase because you do not see the completeness of your true self.

If everything you encounter is perceived as a positive experience, then you would remain an open vessel to attracting positive energy, which would constantly attract positive outcomes in your life. When you are happy and positive, you are infused with the power of growth and abundance. You don't think twice, question, or doubt yourself or your abilities. You contribute to your environment because you add your energies to it. When you choose to allow your environment to adversely affect you, then you are no longer acknowledging yourself and honoring your strength and wisdom.

With these principles in mind, the real definition of the term "free will" is how long you are choosing to attach to your past experiences that continually affect your current life and limit your potential for spiritual growth. If life is impermanent and forever changing, you are the independent variable within a multitude of uncontrolled events occurring all around you. You choose how you want to participate in life and whether or not you want to keep up with yourself and the development of your growth. Your potential is infinite, but you limit yourself with your mental illusionary constraints. You imprison yourself mentally from free will—the freedom from attachments. What is detrimental to you is what you have personally attached to and have deemed of great importance; but in life, the greatest deeds of good will or ill will eventually fade into the past. All that is needed is time.

To know the measure of your own worth is to experience the impact that you make in your life. The way you choose to participate is completely up to you. You choose to experience your life on a regular basis. To add to your surroundings creates growth and empowerment, both for yourself and the people around you. When you allow your personal attachments to control your life, you drain your own energy and hold yourself back mentally and spiritually. To be free of mental attachments and false control is the true act of "free will." This allows you to synchronize harmoniously with the abundance of energy that the universe and life has to offer. To live with freedom from emotional anchors provides for constant growth and expansion and allows your spirit to penetrate your physical existence. This is a road that few have chosen to travel. Let us find out more about the road less traveled on the roadmap to enlightenment.

CHAPTER 18

THE ROAD
LESS TRAVELED

To understand what it means to be enlightened, you must first imagine what it would be like to live in your own divinity. You realize your full potential like others have before you. Awakened consciousness is a difficult task for anyone to achieve, and most people cannot fathom or perceive what it feels like to be enlightened. Yet, millions of people all around the world experience small glimpses of what it feels to be enlightened. They catch a glimpse when they reach moments of clarity in themselves, often as they resolve difficult situations in their life. It feels freeing. Those who have come to know this level of existence radiate it vibrationally for others to feel and sense within their presence.

Take a look around. Why do you see some people living their life without a care or struggle in the world, achieving success so easily in everything that they do? Why do others live in constant turmoil and continually struggle to make ends meet? Why are some people happy without the need of validation, while others eternally strive to accumulate more and more wealth, notoriety, identity, and still manage to be unsatisfied or miserable? Enlightenment can be measured in many different ways, for it evolves within you as you evolve your spiritual and mental abilities. Enlightenment is not your end goal but in many ways is only the beginning of experiencing your spiritual totality. To understand this is to understand what enlightenment has evolved into.

Enlightenment is a state of being, a state of presence in the knowing and awareness of creation and existence. All things have dimensions, but all things also have a beginning. Where you are in your present level of consciousness is an expression of just one aspect of your spiritual dimensions. Consciousness is merely the learning process of knowing and accepting the dimensions of your own presence. In doing so, you expand yourself each time you learn and accept another dimension within yourself, thus your consciousness expands. Through full acceptance of yourself and who you are, you create acceptance within others. Everything has a beginning. From the beginning, there is only expansion. Hence, enlightenment is only the beginning of existing in a state of total awareness and acceptance of your spiritual divinity. Once lit up or brought into existence, you can only expand into what you were meant to be—the presence of your spiritual totality. To know and understand something is only one dimension of understanding. To experience and feel it within yourself completes the knowledge of wisdom through your experiences.

Most of us are extremely happy when we achieve success in life. When we get a promotion or earn a college degree, we feel good about ourselves because we have earned something tangible. These things can define success for us and to others around us. Our achievements are an accumulation of our life experiences based upon decisions and actions that we chose for ourselves. We believed these things would add to us or help us achieve life-altering goals. So why, after achieving numerous goals, certificates and awards in our lives, do we often still feel dissatisfied, unfulfilled or incomplete? Why do we find ourselves headed down new paths, always chasing the next best thing?

When you race after tangible achievements, you have to ask what is motivating you to do this. Do you really need this in your life? Does this increase your wisdom, skill, or education? Or does the answer lie in acquiring validation, labels or increased attention? The answer may be that you are dissatisfied within yourself. Striving for success is good for the spirit if it adds to your life and is not done for the approval of others. If you are seeking approval for your life, whether it is approval from yourself or another, then you may be trying to fill a void of non-acceptance, resistance or emptiness that you have not acknowledged within you.

This maybe true even when you are trying to help other human beings. You sometimes get so caught up in acts of kindness that you lose sight of the reason why you began doing them in the first place. Doing good deeds in order to make you feel good about yourself or fill a void within you can become as addictive as doing drugs or alcohol; it becomes an addiction of approval. It can be a habit that allows you to feel good about yourself, but in truth, is an external attachment rather than an expression that resonates from the core of who you are. Would you feel the same about yourself if you take away the expression of good will? Or would you feel less satisfied with who you are? Whenever you constantly search for goals to accomplish, you may feel a sense of emptiness or uselessness when the goal is taken away. You feel that you have no purpose for being you.

Ask yourself, "What is my passion?" Then, look at the answer. Are there multiple answers, only one, or none at all? Is it something that forces you to rely upon your outer world to make you happy or can you do it by yourself without anyone's approval or acknowledgment? Does this passion feed the desire of your emotions or is it about learning and improving yourself? Remember, there are many ways to measure success. Based on your perceptions, you may measure it professionally, socially or personally. The basis of your measure should never rely on someone else's opinion or even on your own judgment. When you place judgment upon yourself, you are not in acceptance of yourself and are doomed to travel down a road that ends in discontent. This is why the first step toward achieving enlightenment always begins with you.

To understand what it means to be happy is to ask, "What do I want for myself?" The answer to this question reflects your current level of consciousness. Everyone resonates at different levels of consciousness at any given time. What one person perceives as fun or enjoyable is not necessarily what another person sees as entertaining. The things that motivate you or make you happy may not always be things that you know are good for you. Within your many different experiences, you can find something that makes you happy, but what some define as happiness, others label as torture.

Your emotional perceptions dictate your reactions to your experiences. Some people are stimulated and emotionally supported and empowered by being around large groups of people or friends. Others prefer solitude, silence and time to themselves. What is fun and exciting for some maybe exhausting or boring to others. To be content with or without emotional stimulation or support shows the degree of acceptance, strength and comfort you have for yourself. To remain unaffected and independent of external energetic emotional stimulation, outward attachments, is to find true peace and happiness within you. You are able to exist within the freedom of your own presence.

The next question you must ask is, "What am I willing to do to achieve such freedom?" The challenge is to accept yourself as whole and not neglect parts that you plan to deal with later. To live in self-acceptance is to live with unconditional acceptance of all things, no matter what the attachment or consequence. When you see yourself judging or opinionating, then you must look at the part of you that you don't accept. Whenever you blame someone or something else for your problems, you must remember that you have chosen to experience a situation that is independent of you. When you examine every part of your life to see what supports you and what hinders you, you see that you attract the level of your present consciousness resonation. When you identify with things that cause you to sacrifice part of yourself in order to exist in your chosen environment, you have chosen to live with mental anchors and self-built prisons. Learn to know what you value or don't accept within yourself and you will be free to be you.

The basic understanding of enlightenment begins with compassion, respect, and honoring of one's self. In doing so, you do not attach to the illusions that are self-created or self-inflicted. Every decision you make is one of your own choice, and it is independent of the outcome. The only thing you control is how you want to view the world. Your mental limitations or boundaries determine the speed with which you advance towards enlightenment. With any goal you set in life, it begins with a strong desire or devotion towards achieving what you want for yourself. The level of your desire must match the energy level of the end result of the journey.

Your conditioned upbringing as well as your exposure to different experiences widens or narrows your perception within the boundaries of your judgments or beliefs. This begins to lay the foundation of your character and helps to define who you are; however, this is only one dimension of your full potential. To truly define who you are, you must remember that you are connected to a part of everything vibrationally—essentially limitless. Without the conscious awareness of that which you are, you limit your potential within the boundaries of your human existence. By understanding your potential at every level of consciousness evolvement, you are able to define the experience and relate it to yourself within your consciousness so that you can direct the energy flow of your life.

When most people are asked what they want in life, they usually list money, love, family, good health, peace, and happiness. Nearly all of us have declared, "I want to be happy!" Yet few can truly say they have achieved lasting happiness. It is said that happiness is found from within, because the only person preventing you from being happy is you and the limitations of your perceptions. The positive or negative experiences that you energetically attach yourself to is what binds you to your past and prevents you from achieving "happiness" in your life. The word "happy" is an energetic expression that is created by feeling good about your experiences. You choose when you want to experience joy or suffering. An attachment is simply an exchange of energetic information or dialogue to your experiences. Pain and suffering can have the same emotional attachment as joy and bliss – it is a high form of energy. When you attach to an emotion, whether it is perceived positively or negatively, the attachment creates additional mental-emotional energy that provides fuel for you to benefit from. This energy is then processed and interpreted by the ego.

If there was no perceived benefit from feeling your emotions, you would easily let go of the emotional memory or energy of the experience. Rather, the condition of your emotional attachments is directed outwardly: *If I could only achieve this or do that.* All of these "ifs" are simply acknowledging what you don't have or lack in your life in order to feel mentally complete. You have placed mental limitations on yourself, stemming from a sense of lack not only in your life, but also in yourself. So what if you do get this or achieve that? Wouldn't you simply replace *this* or *that* with another *what if*, continually chasing the illusion of your need to feel happy?

When you look towards your outer world to fulfill or satisfy something within yourself, you must first ask what it is about you that you are dissatisfied with and then reflect on the reasons why. When you reject certain aspects about your life, you judge your perceptions, which presents within your mental thoughts as attachments. What you don't accept in others can reflect what you aren't willing to accept within yourself. The need to feel superior within the self reflects outwardly to your environment and to those around you. This causes separation between you and your environment. Remember that we all start with the same basic needs of our animalistic ego. Depending upon how far you have advanced, you can see that the views of other people's experiences are similar experiences that you might have already accomplished or still need to overcome within your life. Essentially, these are things that you have either learned or need to still learn if you have yet to accept them within yourself. The reality of your physical life is whatever experience that you choose to express for yourself, hence the expression of "free will." Your willingness to choose however you want to experience your life is based upon your level of understanding and acceptance within the self. This awareness and understanding is what directs your interaction within the experience—how you perceive, react to and learn from your life experience.

To experience life itself is to direct it in whatever direction you decide that you want life to look and feel like. You choose what experiences of joy or pain you want to embrace. You choose however short or long of a period of time you need to experience, until you are finally able to let go. It is like playing the major role in a big budget film, where you are the main actor and the director at the same time. You feed off your experiences through your mental attachments. You choose them to draw and learn from so that they can add to your knowledge and empower yourself to become a better individual within your wisdom and experience. How you interact within your life is up to you and is either dependent or independent of others. The choice is yours. When you look at an instance in your life, you can view it in many different ways. Your perceptions and judgments are constantly being changed and remolded as you experience life. Remember that your perspective changes depending on the level of consciousness you currently resonate. Your reality is only as real as the current moment you are in.

Life is constantly moving forward, just like time in your virtual paradigm of existence. You can choose to stand still in your mental time or remain in your past through the attachments that you choose. The multi-dimensional universe and the physical world are eternal and infinite. You can even reverse time itself when you choose to stand still for however long you may desire. To understand that this physical world is forever infinite and impermanent helps you to understand that attachments to the illusions of your physical life are no more real than that of an instance. Hence, your life is a temporary illusion. What you do and achieve in your physical life is merely an expression of your spiritual vibrations.

You can stop and challenge the question of the true reality of life, but life still moves forward when you choose to stand still. You can perceptually live and breathe in your physical life, but you will still mirror your spiritual vibrations. It is you who chooses to advance your levels of consciousness. To truly impact your physical life is to develop and grow your spiritual vibration, and this attracts what is necessary for your growth through the physical experience. Your spirit is eternal and all knowing. It has existed long before this lifetime. Your consciousness is working towards the awareness of your spirit that awaits you at the end of your physical life. The information within your present life adds to the wisdom of your spirit into the next life, providing for further expansion and expression within the existence of your spiritual dimensions. Focusing your life from within allows the external experience to come forth and teach you how to grow and move forward within this present life.

What may be correct or perfect at one point in your life may not always be right for you as you advance. To cling to your old truths is to remain stalled in your past. The best course is to be unattached. In doing so, you stay open to new growth and new ideas as they come and go. Like sponges absorbing knowledge, children enjoy learning every new experience in their life. As you grow beyond childhood and are taught to accept your social paradigms, you enter into social judgments and form mental boundaries. The mental mind is a blank computer ready to run whatever program you choose. Your limitations, judgments and boundaries are merely programs directed by your mind, which is controlled by emotional programs within your mental need to control. Your need to control is a large program that you can either continue to run or choose to stop once you realize the lessons within your attachments. Only you can stop the program, because you are the programmer of the fantasies or illusions that fuel your reality.

If you find yourself saying, "That's easier said than done," realize that you are only empowering a false notion that is attached to blame. You are relying on the outer world for your approval or denial of existence. Your choices create your dependency on your attachments or your freedom to learn and grow from your experiences. Your outer world is there for you to learn and grow, and you make best use of it by learning to flow with this physical illusion that is impermanent. Attach to the experiences of your physical world and you slow down the opportunities for your spirit to grow. The physical and mental parts of the self, the mind and body, do not need anything. They are not dependent upon anything other than the need to exist, which directs you to eat, sleep and procreate for evolutionary survival. When you understand that their true purpose is to be the physical vehicle for your spirit to experience, develop and grow, then you become free to engage in your experience without attaching to false needs and desires.

Buddhism teaches you that the path to enlightenment requires you to deny the self and all egoistic desires, because your human existence and any form of the self is considered to be unreal. But how many Buddhist are enlightened today? How many Christians are saved? How many Hindus live in dharma or have reached Brahman? All these religious paths deny one or many parts of the self, which denies your spirit to be present. If you live your life at this simple level of existence, then you follow the path of denying the self and return to your original form from when you entered the physical existence. The original messages have been distorted through time as each religion developed. Adopt the practice of prayer, meditation or living your life in a higher spiritual manner to live your life with a greater understanding of your experiences, not to deny or reject them. To understand this is to come full circle in obtaining higher consciousness; you realize that your spiritual growth relies on the existence and unconditional acceptance of your experience within your unfolding and creation of life.

The Bible states that God created man in his own image, after his own likeness. If there was such a thing as only one God, then why are we not all alike? The person standing next to you may be taller, shorter, male, female, a father, a mother, or a child. We are all different in the way we look, act and perceive things within our thoughts, beliefs, and actions. So ask yourself, if you were God, why would you create so many variations of yourself if you are already perfect? How do you know you are not already perfect? How do you know that God is not inside of you, is a part of you? How do you know you are not a part of God?

Not understanding and comprehending that you are an expression of God can lead to internal conflict and confusion inside of you. With this said, you may struggle with feelings of anger or find resistance with the idea that you are God. It might challenge you to know that the omnipotent God that you may believe in might not exactly exist in the way you may perceive him or her to be. Some of you may want to argue this point. Some of you may want to believe this to be a theory or a lie that challenges your present truth and consciousness, and some may feel and experience emotional resistance to what you have just read. These are all expressions of rejection, resistance, and negativity held within the non-acceptance of your spirit. Negativity attracts, supports, and manifests the expression of violence to come forth. Violence is not what the intended teachings of Masters Jesus, Buddha, or God wanted for you in creating your life.

All the violence in the world is a conglomerate present state of one person's awareness that others either support or disprove. No matter what happens, no matter how great the pain, violence, or suffering we may all be experiencing, all you need to do is close your eyes and sit still in moments of silence. And within a blink of an eye, a whispering second, the thought, emotion, or act has already past, unless you continue to choose to fuel the energy of negativity with your emotions. You hold onto energy in the emotion of your illusionary self until you are able to move on and allow it (or life) to pass by. Within the silence, free of emotion, you return to a state of what God, Enlightenment, Brahman has always taught us: to love and accept all things unconditionally. When you can know God consciousness in yourself, then you will know God and you will know you are a part of God. You return to where you were meant to be, enlightened, "within the light," the experience of who you truly are.

In order to take the next step in your level of understanding and acquire the next level of consciousness, you must first ask yourself what you are experiencing and whether you are truly willing to rewrite your program. Every level of consciousness has a specific program to teach mental awareness and understanding in the human experience. Chakra bodies, the energy centers within you, are the programs you empower and turn on within your mental constructs that tell the mind and body to exist at each level of awareness. Every level of consciousness has a different program for you to experience, and attracts the karmic lessons within each level of resonation. The human body is the shell or computer, your chakras are your programs, and the experience is the medium that creates the mental illusions in your mind when you run your programs. What program are you running in your life today? Is it the program that you want to live? And if it is not, are you willing to upgrade to the next level of understanding that will allow you to operate more efficiently within your life?

To achieve enlightenment, you must ask, "What am I willing to give up in order to gain infinite potentiality?" If you look back at your life, you can see that when you gained knowledge, you usually acquired a better understanding to add to your existence. When you know more, you expand your understanding and improve your experience of life.

Sometimes a skill can be frustrating to learn or a body of knowledge difficult to comprehend, but as you continue to challenge and expand yourself while remaining open, what was once considered difficult becomes natural. No matter where you are in your life, there is always room to learn, grow, and experience the many dimensions that you have to offer to yourself and the world. You are spiritually connected to everything that God and the universe has to offer. God and the universe are within you.

CHAPTER 19

WELCOME TO THE JOURNEY

With the information in this book, you now have a new model and approach to understanding and developing your spiritual consciousness in relation to today's current level of understanding. Your spiritual development is interconnected and has been explained with a modern approach and more current information about spiritual teachings, science and the human vibration. It is an approach that we, as a society, have evolved into. Integrating the information found in these separate disciplines provides you a clearer understanding of your spiritual evolvement.

Your journey towards obtaining higher consciousness begins within you. Levels of enlightenment are achieved as you master the levels of consciousness held within your lower chakra system. As you assimilate the information stored within each level, you learn and understand yourself through the teachings of your spirit within your physical experience. As you raise your human vibration to match the power and frequency of your spiritual presence, you become aware of the light within you. This light shines in the darkness and allows you to see. You become aware of the power and presence of unconditional love and acceptance—the presence of God. Within that higher state of awareness, you come into a new level of existence. You exist as your true self. You exist as the light of your spirit.

Your spirit has evolved with each lifetime. Consciousness on Earth has evolved with the passing of each millennium and the addition of each new spiritual teaching. Although few of us have reached the state of enlightened awareness, with the experience of each new life, your spirit expands the expression of its dimensions. As you move from one experience to the next, you acquire wisdom and continue to learn from lifetime to lifetime. You must experience life to learn and move forward in your spiritual development and understanding of creation and existence. You cannot master yourself until you come to know and fully *experience* yourself. In denying or rejecting parts of your spirit, you create confusion along your path to spiritual awareness. Your spiritual expression becomes only a fragment of its potential presence. Advancing only parts of yourself causes you to stifle your spiritual growth, only to bring you back to the beginning. This can create frustration and confusion within yourself, because you experience separation within your spirit.

When you search for answers to spiritual evolvement in existing literature, spiritual philosophies or in religious teachings, you find that there are interpretations of the beginning and abstract expressions about the end. The result? With a partial and disjointed understanding of your path, you find yourself down a road of continually seeking and following more and more dead ends; you become lost and even more confused. Feeling discouraged can cause you to momentarily give up. You came from something, so you innately know and sense that there is something greater out there. Some look to God, Buddha or some unidentified spiritual source to magically provide them with all the answers. But within the wisdom of silence, the vibration of creation, you come to the realization that this thing that you know and feel to be much greater is not found out there. You find that this greater something exists inside of *you*.

Every path of spirituality has a general set of rules and instructions that point you in the right direction. However, following general guidelines will give you mediocre results. You are a special person, a perfect expression of creation; therefore your path to spiritual awakening is specific, unique, and individual to you. Achieving a level of greatness within yourself requires you to do your own work.

By nurturing your spirit, you support your consciousness development and allow it to unfold naturally. It is very similar to a flower bud. Nurtured with sunlight, water and nutrients from the earth, the bud unfolds at its own pace towards the expression of its beauty. You cannot hasten the flower's unfolding, but you can provide the appropriate nurturing for it to reveal the full beauty of its expression. If you are here to find your true self, you must begin to nurture yourself. You must choose to engage in a relationship with yourself that allows you to unfold. As you begin to increase your consciousness, you know and feel when things are out of balance within you. You can then consciously choose how fast you want to advance by recognizing where you are in your consciousness. You are able to identify your energetic imbalances and work towards harmony with yourself and your environment.

In taking the first step towards higher consciousness, you begin the journey of climbing up the mountain. There are many paths that enable an ascent toward the summit. Some paths are clear and well traveled, while others are uncharted and sometimes frightening. Even if your path leads you down an impassable road that causes you to backtrack or turn around to redirect your course, you can still choose to continue the journey. Each time you attempt to scale the mountain, you do so because you trust in yourself—your spirit. Some may decide to turn back until they are more ready, while others will stop to enjoy the view along the ascent. Teachers and guides will arrive with perfect timing to assist you. Near the top, you find those few who have stayed the course and maintained their devotion with determination to experience their weaknesses and strengths. At the peak of the mountain, all you have left is to take in the beauty and awareness that life has to offer. Within the knowledge of your experience at the end of the journey, you take in the majesty of the awe-inspiring horizon and the results and memory of your achievement: the experience of the self and what it means to you.

The beauty of any significant achievement inspires you to share the knowledge and experience you acquired along your journey. There are many choices along the path down the mountain, the path of sharing and inspiring others to continue their own journey towards the peak of their consciousness. All masters and teachers share the joy of their experiences and what it meant to them as they ascended their consciousness along their chosen path.

In the journey of life, you can only experience yourself. Whether you choose to feel joy, heartache, pain, or suffering along the journey, you choose to experience life, the physical existence. As you advance yourself, you uncover more and more pieces of the puzzle. In learning to unfold the spirit in order to reach the highest expression of yourself, you are able to see what many masters have tried to describe throughout the centuries—you see yourself. When you have finally finished seeking, when everything seems to be failing all around you, all you truly have left is the self and the true power and strength within your own presence.

When we survey the older paradigms of higher consciousness, enlightenment, and salvation, these models of consciousness are based upon a path of rejection. They ask you to reject the ego, thoughts, emotions, and sin. Rejection creates the path of pain and suffering. They ask you to reject yourself. The creation of rejection allows for negative vibrations to exist inside of you and creates resistance within yourself and others to reject the world around you. This negative vibration creates the existence of violence, hatred, judgment and separation that creates the war of consciousness inside you to express itself outwardly. We see the war of lower consciousness everywhere in the world today.

The new path of higher consciousness is a model based on unconditional acceptance leading to unconditional love. When you have complete acceptance within yourself, you have acceptance of the world. You accept your ego, thoughts, and emotions and trace them to their point of origin. In this, you know what you are capable of and then you have the choice to walk another path without resistance. You allow the vibrations of love, compassion, patience, and tolerance to exist within you. These positive vibrations create and support the growth of love and nurturing within you and everyone around you. You feel the connection of the family of God. Being one with the universe or with God is no longer the expression of enlightenment or salvation. Enlightenment has evolved into accepting the expression of an expanding universe. The universe as we know it today is a multi-verse, a universe of dimensions upon dimensions. Your spirit is now capable of evolving into a multi-dimensional spirit. It has evolved into a higher consciousness within you. Higher consciousness has evolved into a complete vibrational expression of multi-verse consciousness versus universal consciousness. We need to learn and accept a multi-consciousness within the world today by accepting it within ourselves first—complete union.

The upper realms of higher consciousness do not judge or get angry when things are not "right" or are out of balance. Higher consciousness accepts everyone at every level in his or her own experience of the self. Consciousness can be measured and can be defined. Of course, there is more to consciousness then what you have read in this book, but the beginning of consciousness starts with you. We are all untapped consciousness, waiting to unfold. When I look at every person around me, I see millions and millions of masters waiting to unfold. There is a master waiting within you. As Master Jesus said, "You are all capable of all that I have done and much, much more." What the great masters achieved in their day was much more than anyone could have imagined or had accomplished for their time and their people. What you are capable of today is much more for your time and your people here on Earth. Many of us have lost our way. You can assist others by simply turning on your own light and raising your vibration to the level of your true capabilities. Become that which you were prior to entering into your physical experience. You are the presence of God. There is no darkness where there is light and in the light we were meant to be. Life is simply a journey of reconnecting back to who you are on the path to enlightenment and beyond. I hope you enjoyed the information held within this book. I am honored you have chosen me to be a part of your path in knowing enlightenment. Remember, when the master stops asking, stops seeking, she finally knows herself.

Welcome to the journey towards discovering who you really are.

THE NEXT STEP

HOW TO ACCELERATE CONSCIOUSNESS GROWTH

s you begin to understand your spiritual evolvement through the chakra system that is a part of your physical and spiritual self, you will see a pattern that takes place within the development of everything in existence. Everything and everyone is at a specific place within their own spiritual evolution. *Roadmap to Enlightenment: A Guidebook to Finding Your True Self* has outlined the progression of spiritual development that we are all experiencing within our physical existence. There is more to you than your physical existence, which makes up only one third of the triune that is known as God or your spirit. You now have the missing steps that must be experienced on the path to achieving "God" within you. Whether you are Christian, Buddhist, Islam, Hindu, or simply seeking a greater spiritual or personal connection, *Roadmap to Enlightenment* gives you a guide to measure where you are at within your own physical-spiritual progression. With this information, you can learn to focus and direct your energies in order to advance or accelerate your physical-spiritual growth.

This is a true guidebook for you to measure where you are at in your own conscious awareness. As you read this material, you begin to create a connection with your spirit on an energetic level. The energy of your thoughts, feelings, and emotions that is generated while reading this material expresses the current energetic frequencies that exist within you. As you read, the thoughts, feelings, and emotions that you create and experience provide a snap shot of where you are in your present level of consciousness. Your emotional reactions to this material, whether positive or negative, become a tool to measure where your current level of consciousness and understanding resides.

Ask yourself, "Do I find myself resisting the material and experiencing negative emotions, or do I easily accept this knowledge?" Negative emotions or resistance are an indication that your level of consciousness is lower than the high level of consciousness and awareness of this material. Understanding where you are at in your consciousness will allow you to redirect your focus and intention towards the next level of consciousness along your personal path to enlightenment. The development of your spiritual consciousness is, in essence, a personal relationship of knowing your true self. Within any personal relationship, you experience the various dimensions that mirror the self and all that it has to offer.

In my next book, I will show you how to accelerate your spiritual growth to higher states of consciousness. It is possible to speed up your spiritual development so that you come to know and experience what you truly are within this lifetime. You can advance regardless of where you are in your present level of consciousness. I will introduce a powerful new form of meditation that allows you to increase and accelerate your human vibration through the levels of your spiritual consciousness. This meditation goes beyond relaxation and clearing the mind to refocus your energies towards the highest source that is found within you—your real connection to God. From the wisdom and guidance of your own divine source, you learn about yourself rather than a perfection or illusion that exists outside of you. You come to understand the connection between your spiritual energies and your physical life. You learn to connect to your spirit, so that you can accelerate your current level of consciousness to better understand your physical and spiritual existence.

You will also learn about the three layers of spiritual development through the Inner Child, Middle Self, and Higher Self, the triune that creates God within you. Understanding the mysteries and true purpose of this triune, and how it relates to your physical life, will provide you with the keys to your spiritual growth. Finally, you will see how to embrace all that you are, which directs your energy so that it works for you. You can free yourself from the negative experiences that you energetically attach to. This freed energy will allow you to attract the things that nurture you and your spirit's growth: happiness, love, abundance, peace, wisdom, truth. By learning how to accelerate the unfolding of higher levels of consciousness within you, you set yourself on an obtainable path to experiencing your own enlightenment.

ABOUT THE AUTHOR

Born in Saigon, Vietnam and raised in the Pacific Northwest, Dr. Minh Vo has pursued a career in the healing arts that has taken him deep into various fields of alternative medicine. After graduating from chiropractic school in the Bay Area, Dr. Vo returned to the Pacific Northwest to establish a practice in Seattle, WA, integrating chiropractic and energy medicine. On his own quest for spiritual growth and through his work as a gifted healer, Dr. Vo discovered a living map of the mental and emotional origins of consciousness within the human body. He understands his purpose as sharing this knowledge to accelerate humanity's spiritual evolution. Through Dr. Vo's work, enlightenment, knowing and experiencing the greatness of who you really are, becomes achievable within your lifetime. *Roadmap to Enlightenment – A Guidebook to Finding Your True Self* provides a clear explanation of the development of human and spiritual states of consciousness that we all experience on the path of finding the truth of our existence.

Dr. Vo now lives in southern California, where he teaches and continues to write. Visit www.drminhvo.com to find out more about Dr. Vo's work, meditation courses, and seminars